T0270004

1992

Rob Fletcher

1992

The Birth of Modern Football

First published by Pitch Publishing, 2023

Pitch Publishing
9 Donnington Park,
85 Birdham Road,
Chichester,
West Sussex,
PO20 7AJ
www.pitchpublishing.co.uk
info@pitchpublishing.co.uk

A CIP catalogue record is available for this book
from the British Library.

ISBN 978 1 80150 428 7

Typesetting and origination by Pitch Publishing
Printed and bound in Great Britain by TJ Books, Padstow

Contents

1. A Changing Landscape: How did we get here? .9

2. Alive and Kicking: A whole new ball game . . 29

3. Do I Not Like That: Disaster for England . . . 58

4. Europe in Flux: Danish Dynamite reborn . . . 85

5. Can He Kick It? Keepers on the ball 112

6. Money, Money, Money: The summer
   transfer explosion 131

7. The Birth of the Starball: Here comes the
   Champions League 153

8. Golazzo: *Football Italia* arrives on Channel 4 . 178

9. Battle of the Roses: Leeds win the battle,
   United win the war 200

10. Legacy: Where are we now? 233

Bibliography 248

To Dora and Arthur, for all your patience, support and encouragement.

1

A Changing Landscape: How did we get here?

FOOTBALL WAS not invented in 1992. No, football changed in 1992 and paved the way for the game we see today. A perfect storm of political, cultural and economic factors made structural changes that opened up the game. Free movement, heavy investment from rich owners and the proliferation of football on television created a truly global game.

Before this monumental shift, football had been in a decline during the 1980s. Since its post-war heyday, attendances were starting to decline, the quality of football had decreased and there was violence on the terraces. In England, especially, football was criticised by the government and the press, with the *Sunday Times* stating that football was 'in crisis: a slum sport played in slum stadiums and increasingly watched by slum people'. Hooliganism was an epidemic and the tragedies that occurred in the decade, accompanied by some horrendous reporting, created an image of a dangerous game for the average fan.

Before then, in the 1960s and 70s heyday for the sport, mercurial talents ruled the game. The likes of Stanley Matthews, Duncan Edwards, Alfredo Di Stéfano, László Kubala, Francisco Gento and more blossomed in their domestic leagues and had the opportunity to showcase their talents to a global audience during the World Cup. The attacking play shown by those teams enraptured spectators and if their games were shown today, journalists and commentators would marvel at the spectacle.

Pele emerged as a teenage prodigy at the 1958 World Cup and the Brazilian became a superstar at home and abroad. Unlike today, he didn't make the move from his home country to the richer leagues in Europe. He stayed pretty much a one-club man until the bright lights of New York came calling.

These players were like ethereal figures. Creating art on the pitch with their innovative playing styles amid ever-developing systems put in place by coaches who wanted to win and entertain. For the first time, these players were seen on television rather than just the sports pages. Globalisation of the game was well underway. The revolution, as they say, was televised.

Development continued into the 1960s with the World Cup at the home of football, Wembley. It brought a nation together and further increased the exposure of the World Cup as FIFA moved to become a more commercial organisation in the 1970s.

Individual players, as ever, were worth the entry fee to these games, with the likes of Johan Cruyff, Franz Beckenbauer, Gerd Muller, George Best, Kenny Dalglish and Kevin Keegan emerging during the 60s and 70s to become poster stars for the game. Merchandising deals became much more common and players supplemented their income off the pitch. There was, of course, no huge backlash to this as there is now because football still mattered, and they weren't all millionaires to begin with.

Off the pitch, managers started to increase their levels of fame too. In England, the likes of Bill Shankly, Brian Clough and Don Revie provided sound bites that were a broadcaster's dream. Coupled with that, they had success to back up their many opinions, becoming successful at home and abroad. That success began in Europe in the 1960s when Manchester United, Liverpool, Leeds and more brought home continental trophies.

During the 70s and into the 80s, English teams truly had a monopoly on the European Cup and dominated the game on the continent. The tactical organisation and quality throughout the teams was too much for others to handle. It was also a decade of relative parity across Europe, as a whole range of teams contested finals, from Hamburg to Malmo.

Before then, multiple clubs had won multiple titles in Europe's premier competition. Real Madrid in the 1950s, Benfica in the 60s and Ajax at the start of the 70s: these clubs had superb individuals but it was not a representation of the league's strength. For the most part, they were triumphant at home, which continued to ensure they were represented in Europe's premier competition.

Down the years, clubs like Manchester United, Liverpool, Real Madrid, Barcelona, Juventus, Inter, Milan, Bayern Munich and Ajax have been the forces that swept aside any challenger. And if a challenger did come into view these big clubs would simply retool and strengthen their squads.

League football always had these dominant clubs that defined eras. They were the big names in each domestic league, fighting for every trophy and developing (or buying) the best players. Often, they provided the spine of the national teams. It allowed these individuals to develop as a collective and experience more success. With success comes the desire to stay at the top and as the game expanded, more clubs wanted a piece of the success on offer.

Football was successful the world over, with huge participation numbers and high viewing figures on television. Domestic games were now becoming part of TV schedules and in England the FA Cup was known the world over for its competitive games and shock results. This appetite for football allowed the game to continue to spread at a rapid rate with World Cups now becoming huge television events, offering host countries the chance to benefit.

The World Cup in Mexico in 1970 presented a game in full technicolour glory. Vibrant kits, crowds and the lush green pitches made the game glow. The truly superb individuals and teams playing during this time are some of the best the world has ever seen. There aren't many decades where a team that did not win any honours on the international stage are remembered more than the winners; hello the Netherlands and Total Football.

After those first few decades of post-war football and the advent of the European Cup in 1955, football reached a crossroads in the 1980s. As is so often the case, sport follows the political and cultural movements of the world it occupies. So, with the Cold War in full flow, there was a real sense of tribalism in the separation between nations. It was also the start of a period that prioritised the individual. Success would not be measured by the collective spirit or achievements of people, but by their individual status and wealth. This, in truth, was a driver for change in the late 80s and early 90s.

Changes had already started to happen across Europe as the 70s became the 80s. For one, Italy had begun the process of allowing foreign-born players to come into the league. This meant that their league became much stronger technically and tactically as a range of coaches and some of the world's best players arrived: players like Michel Platini, Diego Maradona,

Michael Laudrup and Karl-Heinz Rummenigge to name a few of the stars. Italy also attracted many UK-based players to sunnier climes. Liam Brady, Trevor Francis, Graeme Souness, Luther Blissett, Ray Wilkins and more left the British game to test themselves against the best. At this point, they were also being handsomely rewarded for their work. Money was flowing through the Italian game thanks to families like the Agnellis at Juventus and their Fiat empire. These star players were expected to provide the moments that would win a game, as Serie A was notoriously defensive, more so than any other league, and the football was brutal.

The Italian game had been focused around *catenaccio* which is a defence-first tactical system, credited to Karl Rappan in Switzerland. In his comprehensive history of Italian football, *Calcio*, author John Foot notes its most simple principle: take away an attacker and add a defender. Italian football up to the late 1980s was built on this foundation. Hector Herrera's Inter were the purveyors of this style, achieving huge success in the 1960s which Foot describes as an adaptation of the traditional style that had been used in the decades prior.

As you can imagine, games were low-scoring and defensive expertise was prioritised over attacking freedom.

The cynicism and 'boring' nature of the tactics made enemies of the system, especially when you had international teams like Brazil playing a much more aggressive, attacking style of football. Herrera and the Inter faithful did not care too much as their trophy cabinet bulged during this period.

Italian teams also became known for their fearsome defensive stoppers, combative players who used the rules as flexibly as referees would allow. Their attitude towards the dark arts of defence was one of ultimate commitment and professionalism. The emergence of players like Paolo Maldini and Ciro Ferrara in the 1980s in Serie A provided the template for many a defender as the game became more attack-focused in the 1990s.

This is not to say that Italian football didn't have its creative players. There is a long list of players down the years that provided their supporters with incredible moments. The use of the *regista*, the midfield director, allowed players like Gianni Rivera to excel. Andrea Pirlo in the modern era played the *regista* role superbly as demonstrated by his array of titles won at Milan and Juventus.

The late 1960s, and the understanding that *catenaccio* was not unbeatable, brought a newer, faster-paced brand of football and the proponents of that style who achieved huge success were Rinus Michels' Ajax. He was a disciplinarian who brought a professionalism to the club, so that players would be able to cope with his advanced technical and tactical training regime.

Jonathan Wilson notes in his book *Inverting the Pyramid* that the Ajax players had developed the ability to interchange positions rapidly amidst Michels' constant adaptations to his attacking formula. He notes that their pressing was what really set their team apart from the others of that era. On leaving Ajax, Michels took his ideas and principles to Barcelona, and when joined by Cruyff, won La Liga in 1973/74. His shadow would loom large over some of the developments and successes in the modern era from players to coaches.

If the 1960s belonged to *catenaccio* in Milan and Total Football (*totaalvoetbal*) defined the majority of the 1970s, it would be English teams who dominated the European game as the 1970s became the 80s. Of course, Jock Stein's Celtic and Matt Busby's Manchester United had lifted the biggest honour in European football, but no team had dominated. Since the inception of the European Cup in 1955 there were only three teams who were not multiple winners: Celtic, United and Feyenoord.

Bob Paisley and Brian Clough changed that as their sides were part of an unbroken six-year run of European Cup winners from England. It may be telling that five of those six wins were 1-0, which just seems like a typical English result.

Before then, English clubs had lagged behind their European counterparts in the post-war era, as often players and coaches sought to develop elsewhere. Throughout the previous decades the likes of Jimmy Hogan, Jack Reynolds and Vic Buckingham had innovated tactically on the continent, creating successful disciples to carry on their work. Players such as John Charles and Jimmy Greaves had left for Serie A, where restrictions on maximum wages did not apply.

After the huge tactical changes that had swept through football since the 1950s, managers had started to develop their own style and way of playing. They would pick different elements of other systems and not all were wedded to the famous W-M formation, which was dying out thanks to the systems developed by Rocco, Herrera, Michels etc.

Bob Paisley was part of the 'boot room' created under Bill Shankly's leadership at Liverpool as they rose from the Second Division in the late 60s and built a team and philosophy that dominated the 70s and 80s. Shankly realised that, after European Cup disappointments, building play from the back was the only way to play. Shankly, not a renowned tactician – that was Paisley's area of expertise – identified with the ideas set out by Jimmy Hogan decades earlier. Jonathan Wilson notes that Shankly 'had a belief in control almost as profound as Hogan's'. He certainly developed a side that was possession-based and would not look out of place in today's game.

All of these tactical developments and the implementation of ideas like pressing and playing out from the back were creating a much more cosmopolitan game. Clubs were facing each other on the European stage in three major competitions: the European Cup, UEFA Cup and Cup Winners' Cup.

These challenges were embraced by teams that wanted to succeed. Utilising new techniques and adapting old tactics, with foundations of a national identity, made the club game so rich and diverse.

As the 1990s approached, football had been beset by widespread problems of violence across the main leagues in Europe. Football was changing, and especially in England, hooligan culture had taken over the terraces. Matches were marred by violence. The tragedies at Heysel, Bradford and Hillsborough provided examples of varying degrees of administrative incompetence, violence and political interference and cover-up. There would be changes and these would be far-reaching.

The Taylor Report was the first domino to fall in England. Published in 1990 after the tragedy at Hillsborough, the inquiry was commissioned by Margaret Thatcher's government to find out what had caused 97 football fans to lose their lives. Taylor laid blame at the door of the police, but the scale of the tragedy would not be revealed until many years later, after much persistence and campaigning from the survivors' families and the whole city of Liverpool.

One of the recommendations to arise from the report was the need to improve the quality of stadiums across the country. A large portion of the nation's football grounds were no longer fit for purpose and additional safety measures would be required. The removal of standing areas from all professional grounds was the key strand running through the recommendations, but the government eventually reduced this in 1992, to exclude the lowest two leagues in England.

A move to all-seater stadiums was an effort to improve conditions at football matches. Too often, fans had feared for their safety in huge explosions of violence that really did plague the game in the 1980s. It would come to change the audience who watched football and provide huge growth for the sport in the 90s.

During this period, a different breed of owner was emerging and they could see the potential in football. They were desperate for change. The voices in football were no longer the local boys done good; the men in the boardrooms wanted to sell their product and make money. David Dein (Arsenal), Martin Edwards (Manchester United), Irving Scholar (Tottenham

Hotspur), Phil Carter (Everton) and Noel White (Liverpool) were looking to modernise the English game. They loved football and wanted to make their forays into their favourite sport successful.

These men wanted to change the way the game was run. They wanted entertainment at the forefront, keeping supporters happy by putting a better product on the pitch. It was a time of difficulty for people financially and this often spilled out on to the terraces. All the chairmen could see what was happening in the biggest television market for sports: the USA. It gave them the idea that things could change for the better. They just needed a better sales pitch.

The turning point at the end of decades of change, tactical development and creation of many football superstars was Italia 90. The impact of this tournament was seismic, nowhere more so than on English football.

The new stadiums and the intense and fanatical support in Italy that summer, couldn't hide the fact that the football on show was, at times, dull and dreary. A collection of the world's best players was not supposed to produce football that did not excite fans. The personalities were still there, the talent was still there, but the game was in danger of becoming less of a spectacle. For football administrators, owners and broadcasters, this was not what they wanted.

Italia 90 is still held up for many as the tournament that they remember the most. They remember the kits, the players and the madcap moments involving Roger Milla or Gazza. The reality was a tournament that produced the least number of goals per game of any World Cup. But football is about narrative as well as what happens on the pitch. If anything, the modern game has morphed into a narrative-driven sport, rather than sport that drives the narrative. Whether this is better, or worse, is probably the subject of another book.

One nation that benefited more than most from Italia 90 was England. For a country whose game had been taken over by hooliganism in the 1980s, as well as an alarming decline in attendances, a positive showing in the biggest sporting event in the world was essential. The problem was, there was no real hope that this would happen. Not according to most of the English press and fans, anyway.

When Bobby Robson arrived in the England dugout, his Ipswich side had just won the UEFA

Cup, which cemented English football as the most dominant in Europe. Domestic football was booming, but changes in the boardrooms of the biggest clubs altered the drive and ambition of clubs at the highest level to generate success off the pitch as well as on it.

After a poor Euro 88, Robson's stock was low going into the 1990 competition. Never a good sign for a manager. When information leaked about Robson leaving after Italia 90, and having that next job lined up, the press (and some fans) were incredulous. How could Robson do this to England? Why not remove him from the team now? Questions that needed to be answered, but instead, the England team were galvanised by the noise and battened down the hatches.

The treatment of Robson and subsequent England managers by the press has been a huge issue. Obviously, journalists know what sells newspapers, but for the players and staff involved with these tournaments it can hardly be easy to prepare with so much distraction. Robson certainly felt this pressure throughout this tenure, and it would amplify even further for his successor, paving the way for the current modern obsession of 24-hour news, fake Sheikhs and even phone hacking.

Once the tournament came around, and despite the usual injury concerns, the squad looked strong. England were blessed with some excellent forward players from the top clubs who were much more committed to playing football rather than the kick-and-rush tactics advocated by Charles Hughes. He was the FA technical director in the 1980s and early 90s who endorsed a direct approach to football. Fewer than five passes was the most desirable passage of play, which he put down to research based on top-level games. The research was flimsy, limited and far too selective for any true conclusions to be made. Unfortunately, his ideas permeated the English game despite the talent at some of the top clubs.

John Barnes, Gary Lineker, Paul Gascoigne, Peter Beardsley, David Platt and Chris Waddle were all coming to the peak of their powers. On paper, it looked like England would do well. Integrating such quality into a coherent unit would prove difficult, but Robson had to find a solution somehow. There are, I'm sure, many modern managers who would be able to fashion a system that worked for all these players, with today's focus on positionless and role-driven players. Imagine Pep Guardiola with Barnes and Waddle hugging the touchline, providing the ammunition for Lineker and Beardsley with Gascoigne and Platt working behind them in midfield.

Back to the real world and, in truth, the tournament certainly exceeded expectations for Robson's men. Initially, performances in the group stages stuttered, but England became stronger as the weeks wore on. After initial difficulties, Robson settled on a move to three at the back, which meant some tactical tweaks further forward. It is still one of the best groups of English players to have appeared at a football tournament.

England's performances in the knockout games showed their resilience and determination, with enough flair to secure a win. At home, the country was gripped. Pictures beamed back of England players around the pool in Italy looking relaxed really cemented this group as fan favourites.

World in Motion by New Order was making its way up the charts and football had taken over the nation. It was a heady mix of dance culture and rave scene that was bleeding into the national consciousness. The ghastly excesses of the 80s were slowly seeping away and youth culture boomed. And one thing that the kids loved was football. Here we were as a nation with a team that was about to come within a couple of penalties of a World Cup final.

World Cups make players. This tournament was no different. Stars have emerged to have careers off the back of these events. One player that shone brighter than most was in the England team and on the brink of superstardom: Paul Gascoigne. His life changed forever in the summer of 1990. He would also be one of the main characters in the main storylines of 1992.

Gazza, as he had become, was a fan favourite. His displays for Newcastle and then Tottenham got fans excited about football. A player who had the flair of someone born in South America with the attitude of the kid playing football in the park with his friends. His cheeky persona enraptured viewers and his performances in the tournament were nothing short of outstanding. It was a career-making turn and for the England team, losing in the semi-final did not bring ridicule and scorn but praise and joy.

The team were welcomed back on home soil by what seemed like the whole population. People were falling over themselves to sign up players for commercial sponsorship deals and Gazza was at the forefront. The next 12 months was a whirlwind. Everyone wanted a piece of him and he gave what he could. His form didn't suffer either, continuing to excel under Terry Venables at Spurs.

Football was transformed in England. The country that invented the game had come out of the doldrums. In the wake of the Heysel disaster, English teams had been banned from European competition, which meant the national game suffered while others thrived. That ban was about to be lifted, and now English fans remembered what it was like to experience success against their continental rivals. The game was certainly not in rude health domestically, but this new groundswell of public interest was about to be capitalised on in a way that would transform not only the domestic game but change the outlook of the sport.

This is 1992, the birth of modern football.

2

Alive and Kicking:
A whole new ball game

THE ENGLISH football pyramid is what separates it from leagues across the world. Endless depth with a variety of clubs housed within a myriad of leagues. Having 92 professional clubs is both remarkable and improbable. One of the reasons there is so much fervour for the English game is the sheer number of clubs and fans that follow them.

Similarly, the England national side has had, in more recent years, a core group of supporters that follow the team around the world. Banners with their club allegiances mix with those of rivals as they take to the terraces to encourage players who normally would be their foes. Whether it is qualifying matches, tournaments on other continents or meaningless friendlies, the English fans follow their team.

These two parts of the English game were often exclusive. One did not always help the other and the Football Association felt like they needed to act. The result of countless tournament missteps, for a national team that was on top of the world in 1966 and the gruelling schedule (and style of football) prevalent in the domestic game throughout the 1980s, gave the FA the impetus.

Modern football in England would come to be defined by two documents. The first was the report by Lord Justice Peter Taylor which outlined the move to all-seater stadiums, but also suggested that football should be rebranded, reshaped, and retooled to cater more towards the emerging middle classes, as the boom in commercialisation took hold.

The Taylor Report was commissioned after the tragedy at Hillsborough in 1989. It changed the lives of families in a city that waited a lifetime for justice.

The disaster at Valley Parade and the events at Heysel prompted discussion at all levels of the law and resulted in changes to the game. Football was in desperate need of modernisation to prevent other events like this.

The Taylor Report placed the burden of equipping their stadiums with seats on the clubs. This would prove to be a colossal financial undertaking, despite any government grants of support. Money was certainly not flowing through the game in the same way that it does today. Clubs were much more frugal. They had to be. Clubs would have to find a way to increase their revenue in order to finance the recommendations.

The Taylor Report in 1990 was the first domino to fall in the birth of modern football. The report laid out plans to modernise football stadiums across the country. These dilapidated, run-down buildings would be brought up to date with improved safety measures, better facilities for all and more importantly, all-seater arenas. And it would be the football clubs that would foot the bill. A new, larger source of income was required to fund these recommendations, especially as attendances would be reduced in the short term.

The second defining document was *The Blueprint for the Future of Football* produced by the Football Association in June 1991. The Football Association had realised that all was not well in the domestic game when the document was released. It was the brainchild of incumbent FA director of coaching Charles Hughes, rubber-stamped by chief executive Graham Kelly, and it laid out a vision of a Premier League atop the English football pyramid, bolstered by revenue four times what those clubs commanded at that point.

These two documents paved the way for the changes that have gripped English football, and ultimately created a league that is unrecognisable from the others in the league pyramid and one that now dominates world football financially.

Most clubs were not being run as efficiently and in the most businesslike manner possible during the 1970s and 1980s. As always in many sports leagues, it was the bigger clubs that wanted to maximise their revenue. Often, these big clubs do not think to take note of the world outside of their own. History has a habit of repeating itself.

These biggest clubs – the Big Five, namely Liverpool, Everton, Arsenal, Manchester United and Tottenham Hotspur – started to work on a plan that would mean they broke away from the structures of the Football League, who wielded the ultimate power. This freedom meant they would be able to define terms that would ensure they stayed the richest clubs in the country and which gave them the opportunity to exploit future commercial opportunities. All these things were in short supply in the 1980s, which was a terrible era for football.

Football in the 80s was a hard sell. Matches were often attritional, influenced by Hughes and his work on 'POMO' or 'Position of Maximum Opportunity', a style of play endorsed by the Football Association. Hughes, inspired by Charles Reep, outlined a way of playing that would bring about the most effective results. Who wouldn't want to have this at their fingertips? It prioritised the number of passes it should take to score a goal, from a sample size that would make modern day data analysts cower behind their laptops, and stressed the importance of set plays and crosses into the box.

There were problems of course, but this style caught on, with teams like Watford, Wimbledon and Cambridge embracing this philosophy with huge success. It wasn't the football that fans of the mavericks and hard men of the 70s had been used to.

Now, it was a more physical sport in all aspects. The second ball and 'getting it in the mixer' were never more popular than during this decade.

As with most innovations or coaching manuals, they are not always meant to be taken literally. Hughes's own work made sweeping generalisations about teams and the tactics they should employ. The data was highly selective and had no real relevance to how the game should be played. Plainly, it should never have become a blueprint for how to play football.

This brand of football did not catch on with elite clubs. English football dominated Europe from the late 70s and into the 80s with some excellent sides. The defending was resolute, yes, but the style of play was far from the Hughes model. English teams thrived during this period with some of the best club sides on the continent. They all played a similar system, but the way they executed their game-plan was always too much for the opposition.

However, on-field success brought riches to these top teams, who were then able to reinvest the money they had on more technically gifted players. This was true of the top five English clubs by the end of the decade. Giving these teams more financial muscle was certainly not desirable for the league unless they were going to be compensated too.

Liverpool, Everton, Arsenal, Manchester United and Tottenham Hotspur wanted change. As a group their owners wanted to increase their share of revenue from television. The only way they could see themselves doing this was through a breakaway league. Throughout the 80s, they tried and failed to get the idea off the ground. Various scenarios were discussed, but most involved resigning from the Football League and becoming a separate entity entirely. They started plotting with the idea that they would try and sell their own television rights, now a common practice for lots of clubs in Europe, to maximise their revenue and tap into the huge potential of the live sports audience. They did not want to be mired in the depths of what television coverage of the nation's game had become in the mid-80s.

The decade was a huge period of change politically, culturally and socially. A world that was opening up, a country that was moving towards a new Thatcherite way of life. The hazy days of the 1960s and 70s began to fade. With these changes came new faces in the boardrooms of big clubs. New owners and investors were putting money into football clubs and wanted to profit. They were businessmen and really did not have time for running clubs the way they always had been run. Revenues needed to increase, and clubs were determined to find a way to do it.

Football had always been shown on television. It had come in various forms, in a variety of competitions, but it had always been popular. World Cups had always drawn huge audiences and channels were keen to make sure they had the live showcase for their viewers. Fewer channels also meant a more concentrated audience. They would watch football on these occasions because it was part of tradition.

Clubs and TV companies failed to realise that not having football on air was a disaster. This came to fruition in the 1985/86 season when the unthinkable happened. Football was not shown at the start of the season. No live games, no highlights packages. Nothing. The bleak state of the game off the pitch was reinforced by the product on it. Big clubs were no longer happy to share their television revenue equally with a team languishing at the bottom of the fourth division. A sense of parity and unison as a football league was beginning to erode. Negotiations were tense and difficult. It was clear that not everyone was working with the same goals in mind. Attentions were turning elsewhere. Television companies baulked at the demands of the clubs to suppress the number of live games to preserve matchday attendances and therefore their direct revenue. Clubs were insistent that their product was worth more. Paying more for less never goes down well in a negotiation.

The Big Five met in 1985 amidst the television blackout to see if more drastic action could be taken. Before long, a deal was agreed with the BBC and ITV and football was back on the air. The total cost to the TV companies: £1.3m a season. The cost to the clubs in the Football League: a door opened to a world of individual clubs running riot over future negotiations.

The next television deal came in 1988 and caused carnage amongst football clubs. A close call with upstart satellite company BSB almost made everyone rich, but when clubs realised the new tech was literally pie in the sky they quickly scurried away. Enter Greg Dyke from ITV. He knew that live sport was good value for viewers (the most precious commodity in the television landscape) and tried his hardest to make a deal happen. Rather than making a deal across the whole league, Dyke targeted the Big Five. Remember that the deal signed off in 1985 netted the league £1.3m a season. Dyke offered the top clubs in England £1m each for the rights to their home matches. As you can imagine, this did not go down well with other Football League clubs. Not only had negotiations happened behind closed doors, away from the collective bargaining table, but smaller clubs would be significantly worse off. They would become the forgotten clubs. A hastily created deal was signed at £11m a year with 21 live games to be shown on ITV. The deal was a massive ratings success for Dyke and his channel.

The investment paid off. The climax to the 1988/89 season proved to be a winner with audiences as more than ten million viewers tuned in to watch Arsenal beat Liverpool to the title in the final game of the season. Potential had become a reality and if football could secure viewing figures anywhere near that amount on a regular basis, then a lot of people would become very rich.

At this point, football fans had not become a commodity. They were the lifeblood of the game. A deep-seated love for football was clear from those in attendance. Passion and joy spilled out of die-hard fans as they watched their teams compete for glory. These elements were not enough for the dark side of the game to become the face of the game in the 80s.

Violence was rife. Something had to be done to expel it from the terraces. It was a game with very rough edges. But not everyone went to the match to indulge in tribal violence. At the heart of it, the game was mainly for the working class. The Saturday rituals at the end of the working week kept the 92 league clubs breathing. Crowds would of course change, but at this time football had not yet been sanitised and it was these rough edges that endeared it to the audience. David Goldblatt confirms this in his book *The Game of Our Lives*, saying that the crowd still 'offered a raucous chorus' and the groups players and fans were drawn from were still 'urban working-class'.

These traits are what appealed to television companies in the early 90s. If they could bottle the passionate atmosphere and quash the violence, they could take it to a television audience. The game could be opened not just to the tens of thousands who filled a football stadium, but potentially millions at home.

For the most part in football history, television coverage of teams came in the form of the *Match of the Day* highlights package. Live games were irregular, with owners terrified of losing their paying audience. The lifeblood of football clubs was the fans in the stadium. Television revenue was shared equally between the league clubs and did not amount to anywhere near what clubs received through gate receipts.

Despite the lack of football on the box, showpiece events always proved popular. FA Cup games shown live on TV would bolster clubs' coffers, and the final was always the biggest match of the football calendar. The extensive build-up featuring all manner of events before the actual kick-off had armchair fans glued to their TV set. These one-off games were no threat to club owners. It was merely a way for other fans across the country (and the world) to watch the biggest game of the season. Times were changing, in football, on television and in the boardroom.

So, at a meeting in the autumn of 1991, the Big Five hatched their plan to leave the Football League. It was a bold, brave, and possibly cataclysmic event that could have destroyed English football. Some might argue, at that moment, it did.

The build-up in the press to the possibility of a breakaway league was one of dismay and derision. Quality football was not on offer in England at the time. Most aspects of the game trailed the much wealthier and tactically advanced teams on the continent. It would take much more than a flashy new TV deal to make the English game relevant again.

The *Blueprint for Football* was created by the Football Association with the purpose of improving the domestic game. One of the early proposals was to reduce the top division of English football to 18 teams. The rationale was that it would ensure that players had sufficient rest to allow them to perform at a higher level for England. It would also allow them to fall into line with some of the other leading nations.

A reduction in teams in the league was rejected immediately. Instead, a 22-team league was agreed. Already, the new breakaway was becoming about a desperate desire from all clubs to access the bumper finances that could be on offer.

The Football Association were also enthralled with the idea of a changing nation. In their *Blueprint* they stated their intention to focus on the 'affluent "middle-class" consumer in his or her pursuits and aspirations'. That was the clincher. A statement that would ring in the ears of football chairmen across the country as they targeted their 'product' to people who had benefited from rising property prices and gentrification.

The new league was ratified by the FA and then attention turned to the matter of the small details that would provide the backbone of what the competition would look like. Meeting in March 1992, Rick Parry, the chief executive of the Premier League, led discussions around a wide-ranging set of proposals. Rather than some of the wilder suggestions that always seem to occur around any form of change, the Premier League proposals certainly had merit, even if they did not immediately come into force.

A ten-point plan was drawn up and shared with the prospective Premier League clubs. Amongst the proposals were the number of teams in the league: 22 teams in the first three seasons, before moving down to 20 from 95/96 and using the three-up and three-down promotion and relegation system. Scheduled international breaks to allow players more rest and the idea of a mid-season break were floated, which were already used positively in other leagues. The former has been in force for several years, while the latter has taken a huge amount of time to come to fruition.

Another interesting idea was the restriction of transfers during the season. Letters from fans and endless columns by ex-players shared their annoyance with the constant transfer activity in the league, so this seemed sensible. Of course, there was already a transfer deadline, but it came so far towards the end of the season to be rendered ineffective. This proposal set out a two-week transfer period mid-season, which again, now, seems logical. It would not be one that clubs agreed to.

Eventually, the league agreed a full, detailed structure and it was time to negotiate a new, and potentially lucrative, television deal. There was still a great deal of debate around it, with ideas including games only being shown on TV if they were a sell-out. If there were tickets still available, then it would only be broadcast outside the region. This would have been a policy ITV would have supported thanks to their various regional broadcasting departments around the country.

One thing that Parry knew he wanted from the television deal was more rounded coverage of the league; a wide range of magazine shows that promoted the league and shared behind-the-scenes insight from the clubs. At the time he was keen to point out that the league wanted to 'ensure that all our clubs are able to compete at the highest level in Europe' while also insisting that there would be better facilities for supporters and equality in terms of voting power and revenue sharing. It seemed like a football utopia.

Large companies certainly do not care much for utopia. The battle for the television rights in English football had never got to the point it had in 1992. Historically they were not always seen as the most important part of the game. In that respect, things were about to change dramatically.

The man at the forefront of the negotiations was ITV's Dyke. He had been one of the key orchestrators in support of the Big Five and their desire to break away. Against him this time was the Rupert Murdoch-led BSkyB, who were intent on disrupting the established order. Dyke thought he was in pole position. Murdoch, on the other hand, had something Dyke did not: a willingness to spend recklessly.

At the time, BSkyB was still emerging, as was its subscription-based model of pay TV. Confidence in the model was not shared by many in the football world. There was a huge swell of derision aimed at the new breakaway 'Super League' and the pay television audience it coveted.

Now, the company is synonymous with football and the Premier League. It could be argued that Sky Sports functions as an arm of the league, fuelling transfer rumours, managerial changes and endless scrutiny of teams' play. The close ties with the league and its broadcaster have only got stronger as smaller competitors have come and gone.

To make all this a reality, the clubs, who had wanted a breakaway for a number of years, took to the negotiating table with ITV and BSkyB. Discussions were tense and lengthy. Under the new Premier League rules, a majority of 14 clubs was required to ratify any decision. The one-club-one-vote rule was the democratic backbone that the new league would be built on. It served to give the smaller clubs a voice and left the Big Five on a level playing field – for now.

This being football, the deal was not easy. Dyke felt he had the support of the biggest clubs in the country and the clout at ITV to offer a substantial package. His offer was £262m over five years – an utterly incomprehensible figure in comparison to the paltry packages on offer only years before. Dyke was content. He was in the driving seat.

If ITV had BSkyB on the ropes, the challengers were about to get a pep talk from their corner. And in their corner was the owner of Amstrad, Alan Sugar, who supplied satellite dishes to Sky's customers, and knew that the rights to live football would mean an explosion in new subscriptions. Not content with the eye-watering money on offer, Sugar implored BSkyB chief Sam Chisholm to 'blow them [ITV] out of the water' and that's exactly what they did. The deal was agreed. An incredible £304m had secured the rights for the new Premier League for the next five years.

Incidentally, the deciding vote to ratify the deal at 14-6 (with two teams abstaining), and hand the keys to Sky, came from the newly appointed Spurs owner: Mr Alan Sugar, owner of Amstrad.

The revolution was about to be televised.

The marketplace for football rights was exploding around the continent, with plans in Europe to show more football than ever. In England, Channel 4 signed up the superstars of Serie A and ITV, still licking their wounds, signed up to show regional games from the Football League. Many people did not think the extra expense of a satellite dish protruding from the side of their house was worth it. Convincing the public to sign up for this would be difficult. With the richest league in the world now also on terrestrial TV, it would not be plain sailing.

But Sky thought it would be worth it. Showing 60 live games across the season was unprecedented, but it was the ancillary programmes that would really separate the channel from what the terrestrial rivals had been able to do. Not content with just live football, there would be the aforementioned *Super Sunday* epic show, a two-hour discussion programme on a Tuesday, a 30-minute club feature on a Wednesday, a one-hour programme previewing the upcoming games and a programme with detailed tactical analysis every Thursday. For the price customers had to pay, if you were a football fan, your needs were well catered for.

The BBC were back as the junior partner in the broadcast deal with the return of *Match of the Day* and *Football Focus* in its Saturday afternoon slot. They had not been involved in the initial breakaway discussions, but now they were reaping the benefits of Dyke and the Big Five's actions.

Channel 4 meanwhile swept up those Serie A rights for just £1.5m, an absolute pittance – the equivalent of just ten per cent of Gianluigi Lentini's transfer fee. Having free-to-air football was huge for Channel 4 and the impact of *Football Italia* on the English fan was huge. Eventually, it would have an impact on the way the game moved too as, like Serie A, the Premier League was awash with cash and attracted elite players from around the world.

So, now that Sky had the TV deal in the bag it needed to get around to the business of getting the football into homes. The first thing for subscribers to do was make sure they had a satellite dish marooned halfway up an outside wall of their house. Once they had managed to overcome this hurdle, they were able to settle down on the sofa for bumper preview and review shows which bloated Sky's schedule for years to come. It was a marked shift from the days of barely a live match gracing the living rooms of a nation.

Broadcasting two games a week, one on a Sunday afternoon and one on a Monday evening, drew the ire of traditionalists the country over. In typical US-influenced style, Sky's coverage was bold, brash, loud and distinctly un-British. From Richard Keys' garish jackets to the sumo wrestlers and cheerleaders at half-time, everything was geared towards spectacle. Andy Gray would fill the position of famous ex-pro, as had been a staple on television for years, but took it to another level with a dual role as co-commentator and studio analyst. To their credit, Sky understood that there was a huge untapped market ready to dive into this coverage.

In the commentary booth was Martin Tyler. Having been part of Sky's main commentary team for their 91/92 Serie A coverage, he wrote about the new approach to football on TV in *World Soccer*. He stated that he did not see Sky as an attack on tradition, instead a chance for new traditions to be created. He referenced the US giant ESPN and how they had changed viewers' habits over a long period of time. His employers would be looking to do the same.

Tyler made some interesting points. Football as viewed through the terrestrial lens was limited by the broadcasters' commitment to showing 'programmes of news, religion, politics, current affairs and culture', he said. He believed that there was a gap that football could fill on the schedules and Sky would attempt to do it with their commitment to supersized preview and review shows built around their live coverage.

Now that clubs had additional resources, fans would have hoped they would see this reflected in the quality of play. It took a while for this to really come to fruition, but the green shoots of investment came in summer 1992. Teams did not splurge on a high number of expensive players, but the number of players signed for over £1m increased dramatically. Still, this was peanuts compared to the incredible spending power of Serie A. In England, it would be Jack Walker's millions and not that of the Big Five which broke the transfer record.

After spending over £5m on players to get Blackburn Rovers into the Premier League, local steel magnate Walker was more than happy to bankroll more spending for manager Kenny Dalglish. Having left his job at Liverpool in the wake of the Hillsborough tragedy, Dalglish was enjoying management again and was keen to add to his squad. One player who was in the transfer columns of all the major newspapers was Alan Shearer, then a 21-year-old who had just made his way into the England setup. There was potential there, but nothing on the scale of what he was about to show.

Transfers are notoriously difficult, but crucial to generate fan excitement before the coming season and complete the jigsaw for a manager. Shearer did both. He was about to become the elite striker in the league and enthral fans with his supreme, all-round forward play. However, his passage to Blackburn was not plain sailing; one club had other ideas.

Having capitulated in their bid to win the First Division title under pressure and mounting games towards the end of the 91/92 season, Manchester United and Alex Ferguson knew they were close to ending their title drought. Shearer could be the final piece of the jigsaw. In his usual indomitable manner, Ferguson pursued Shearer relentlessly, convinced he could attract the young star to Manchester. Ultimately, Ferguson's pursuit was in vain as the young Geordie signed for Blackburn at the end of July for a domestic record of £3.6m, eclipsing the £2.9m Liverpool had paid for Dean Saunders. The latter transfer deal hadn't worked out too well for Souness's Liverpool so all eyes would be on Shearer, and the opening day of the season to see if he could deliver.

Of course, Shearer's transfer was not the only major deal; it wasn't the most expensive involving an Englishman either. Paul Gascoigne and David Platt were two English stars who would not be plying their trade in the new Premier League. Platt, having played a part in the relegation of Bari to Serie B, stayed in Italy as he moved to Serie A giants Juventus for £6.5m. Gazza's protracted transfer to Lazio was finally completed, albeit at a reduced price. Initially, Spurs asked the Italian giants for £10m, but this was negotiated down to £7.5m. After the debacle in the FA Cup final, and the tackle on Gary Charles, Lazio re-negotiated the fee to £5.5m.

England's two most expensive players would not be part of the new domestic game, which was a huge loss. It had been the case in the preceding years too as players like Chris Waddle, Trevor Steven and Des Walker were lured away by the footballing (and financial) rewards of playing on the continent. It is unsurprising to hear that Gazza was offered £22,000 a week to sign for Lazio, when his Spurs wage was a tenth of that. The English game was still lagging behind when it came to wages and transfer fees.

Most English clubs spent the summer adding talent to their squads with millions spent in the process. In total, Premier League clubs spent close to £50m – pretty good going for 22 clubs, but when you consider AC Milan and Juventus covered that themselves, the gulf was still huge.

The names were certainly not from the upper echelons of talent with Paul Stewart (Liverpool), Robert Fleck (Chelsea), David Rocastle (Leeds) and Darren Anderton (Spurs) joining Shearer in the top five most expensive signings of the summer. Interestingly, it would be David Rocastle's first of three consecutive summer transfers after spending his first seven years at Arsenal.

The spending in 92/93 made the £1m transfer commonplace. Every year, transfer prices inched up as teams spent their TV-fuelled riches on players. Clearly, the need to maximise the product on the pitch was crucial. Selling subscriptions, shifting tickets that carried a higher price and filling all-seater stadiums was not going to happen with the same product of the old First Division.

Once the money was really flowing through the Premier League and rules around the movement of players relaxed, the floodgates well and truly opened. Players who were handsomely rewarded in leagues across Europe flocked to the Premier League. Clubs could match (and exceed) the financial packages on offer.

Those first years of the Premier League were categorised by a preference for (at times) overpriced English talent, but with the arrival of Jurgen Klinsmann in 1994 and then Ruud Gullit in 1995 the tide really did turn. The glamour once reserved for Serie A had arrived on English shores. Those two players, with their incredible club and international careers, started the shift towards a more outward-looking league. No longer were European stars out of reach; they were courting English clubs to sign them.

This shift towards more continental players was stark. Foreign players made up five per cent of playing squads in 1992, but just over ten years later that had become 60 per cent. Logically, managers from abroad soon followed and this led to a further change in players.

In those 90s years of increased spending, it was not only the Big Five who would compete at the top of the market. Smaller clubs, with increased power in the transfer market, spent their money on their own stars. Just looking down the list of major transfers in the 1990s, you have Middlesbrough who signed Nick Barmby and Juninho in 1995 and then Emerson and Fabrizio Ravanelli in 1996. The total for these players was over £20m, or in essence, the same amount spent by half the league a few years earlier.

Fuelling these transfer splurges was the continued investment in the league from Sky. Every three, four or five years, the television deal expires and more money is pumped into clubs to spend/waste on inflated transfer fees and wages. It has created a product that is watched around the globe. The relentless self-promotion has meant that every country in the world knows teams and players who play in the Premier League.

Still, despite the increase in talent on home shores, the league has continued to have the same criticism levelled at it as it did in its inception in 1992: inflated ticket prices for fans, a league that serves the television channels' agenda and eye-watering sums of money spent on players' wages and agents' fees is still ammunition for the league's detractors.

Has any good come from the league's formation? Well, yes. It just depends on how you view the outcomes and which time you decide to focus on. The 1990s, as the league was rising, was a perfect mix of English traditions with splashes of international players that were maybe not quite at their peak or had talents that were not harnessed elsewhere. The gaping chasm between the financial strength of different clubs was also reduced during that decade and so provided a much more interesting product.

Despite all of this, like Liverpool in the 80s, one team dominated the competition so nothing really had changed too much.

As the league grew, it became almost omnipotent in football thanks to the enormous investment from Roman Abramovich, who made Chelsea a footballing superpower. Really, this was no different to what Jack Walker had done with Blackburn in the early 90s, but Walker didn't happen to be a Russian oligarch. Similarly, as the 2010s arrived it was Manchester City who barged into the race for the top with more investment in a football club and its infrastructure than had ever been seen.

Both of these clubs have brought players, managers and a brand of football that has enthralled supporters of their teams but have also brought a much bigger global audience than ever before to the English game. Really, the league is no longer part of English football, it is a showcase for teams to accumulate wealth, fans and put themselves in the television window around the world.

Writing for *World Soccer* in 1992, Brian Glanville was unimpressed with the idea behind a new top tier. The notion of what he called a 'Greed is Good' league would only serve to create more problems than it would solve in the English game. 'A whole new ball game' was more than just a tagline – it was a window into the future.

3

Do I Not Like That: Disaster for England

TRADITION IN football is everything. From club colours, the crest, stadiums, fans, songs: we default to these traditions to understand the game and our place in it. As time passes, of course, these traditions can erode. New traditions are made, and this book looks at how change occurs and what its impact is. However, there is one main tradition in England that will seemingly never be broken: the persecution of the England manager.

Graham Taylor was born in Worksop but grew up in Scunthorpe. He was brought into football through his father and quickly developed a love of the game. After a playing career that spanned ten years and only two clubs, Taylor made the step up to become a manager due to injury. It's the classic story of a career cut short that drives a single-minded focus to succeed in the dugout.

It all started at Lincoln City, with Taylor enjoying wide-ranging success, culminating in the Fourth Division title in 1976, at the age of 32. Five years earlier, he had been the youngest person to ever become an FA coach; it was clear he was destined for big things. Moving to Watford in June 1977, Taylor was appointed by then chairman Elton John. Taylor spurned the advances of bigger clubs; he could see the potential at Vicarage Road.

So, the scene was set for a rags-to-riches tale of Watford Football Club powering through the divisions with an inspirational young coach, playing a startling and fresh style of football. Not quite. Taylor was certainly young, often inspirational to his players, but the style of football was certainly not what you would call startling. Taylor's Watford side featured a teenage John Barnes, star striker Luther Blissett and target-man Gerry Armstrong. The football the team played was heavily criticised by the media; it was direct, aggressive, fast-paced and Taylor wanted the ball in the goalmouth as much as possible. This was no pass-and-move style that

Brian Clough and Bob Paisley were implementing at home and in Europe.

The system was ruthlessly effective and Taylor's direct brand of football produced a phenomenal number of goals; two seasons with 80-plus goals earned Watford promotion from the Fourth and Third Divisions. It took three attempts to gain promotion from the Second to the First Division, but then 76 goals earned them a second-place finish in the top tier. Set pieces, throw-ins and getting the ball forward as quickly as possible were key facets of the game. Taylor went on record to say that the system was set up to have the most shots possible. If these came in the same passage of play even better.

A problem that arose for Taylor's reputation was the emergence of Wimbledon, who achieved a similar ascent to the First Division. They developed an even more aggressive style of play that slimmed the system down to the bare bones. Unfairly, this tarred Taylor with the same direct, long-ball tag. This would plague his career in the eyes of the football world and his appointment with England. Taylor characterised football as a simple game that he did not want to complicate. Unfortunately, this had tormented English managers and players since the early 70s.

While the England team stumbled through qualification campaigns and tournaments, the domestic game had dominated Europe. English clubs won six consecutive European Cups from 1977 to 1982. It was a truly incredible period for English football, characterised by the teams' unrelenting will to win and the use of players from the home nations. It also served to highlight the weight of expectation that club football brings to the national team. The tactics were certainly not revolutionary, but it was the only period during which English football would feature consistently in European finals until the 2000s.

The 1980s was characterised as a bleak time for the English game. Hooliganism, poor quality football, unappealing tactics and truly awful tragedies meant the game was at its lowest ebb by the end of the decade. Fractious wranglings in boardrooms across the country fuelled speculation of a new super league at the top of the football pyramid. Clubs were acting in their own self-interest, trying to maximise income as attendances dwindled. It was a long way from the late 70s and early 80s. Change was certainly afoot and it came with the World Cup in 1990.

Italia 90 transformed English football. Fans fell in love with the game again, fell in love with England again and most of all showed that football was a sport that could transcend national differences. The tournament also brought Bobby Robson's time as England manager to an end. Through eight years of scrutiny, Robson had emerged with his head held high. A World Cup semi-final penalty defeat would linger in fans' minds, rather than the disappointment of Euro 88 and failure to qualify in 84.

The search for a new England manager began as news broke that Bobby Robson would be leaving the job for PSV Eindhoven. Of course, the story was leaked in the press and Robson was crucified, to the point that a press conference was called to release the story. Clearly, the next man would not have a straightforward task.

Graham Taylor was the man for the job. Having left Watford for another project at Aston Villa, Taylor was not a popular choice. He achieved promotion at the first time of asking, and then finished second in the First Division. This time the football was different to Watford. Similar principles, but with more talent.

A whole host of criticisms swirled; he's never played in the top flight, he's never won a trophy, his football is too direct. These tactics had been softened at Aston Villa and he'd created an exciting, attacking side with England star David Platt as the centrepiece. That didn't stop the detractors, who surfaced quickly. Capitalising on the success of Italia 90 was difficult for any manager, but for Taylor it seemed that he already had an impossible job on his hands.

Robson had left England on a high. The fans were back on side and the players, despite some questionable early performances, were a talented group. Players in their prime, performing for top clubs at home and abroad. Paul Gascoigne had become a star, Gary Lineker was still scoring goals for fun and Chris Waddle, Peter Beardsley and John Barnes provided the flair and skill alongside the goals of Platt. It seemed an easy task for Taylor to continue the journey.

Despite the reservations of the press and fans, Taylor began his tenure at Wembley against Hungary. He selected a team that could quite easily have been selected by Robson. Chris Woods, then of Rangers, stepped in for the retired Peter Shilton and Lee Dixon came in on the right side of defence in a back five. Steve Bull was preferred in attack to Peter Beardsley and Chris Waddle had to make do with a place on the bench. England won 1-0 thanks to a Lineker goal. So far, so good.

Looking down the team sheet, the ages of the players were almost perfect in terms of tournament preparation. Players aged 23 (Gascoigne) to 30 (Woods) meant they should have been primed and ready for a push at the European Championships in 1992. It certainly would not turn out that way and one of the major factors behind the problems within Taylor's reign was the sheer volume of players used in his squads.

England were handed a generous draw for the Euro qualifiers: Republic of Ireland, Poland and Turkey providing the opposition. Taylor's side were expected to progress, comfortably, and maybe even with some style. The opening qualifying game featured the same side that had beaten Hungary. A Lineker penalty and a superb strike from outside the box from sub Beardsley gave England the win. Roars at the final whistle greeted the England team; they believed that after the exploits at the World Cup it was a team on the up.

Difficulty followed soon after, with England struggling to navigate their way through the qualifying matches. They were hard to beat, winning three and drawing three of their games, but mustered a measly seven goals in the process. Part of the reason was Taylor's inability to find the right balance in the side and his refusal to hand freedom to the squad's most creative players, never more so than during his third match in charge, at Lansdowne Road against the Republic of Ireland. After the highs of Italia 90 and becoming the most sought-after player in world football, Gazza found himself sitting on the bench. Taylor, at the time, said that he didn't want England's number eight in the side due to the possible bruising nature of an encounter with Jack Charlton's well-drilled side. Gordon Cowans took his place. It was not received well. Despite Cowans' ability and impressive performances in the First Division, he was no Gazza and was not the kind of player who could unlock an organised defence. Similarly, the use of Steve McMahon in the midfield was more cautious than creative.

The media, despite Taylor's very open manner, were quick to question his selections and this continued with the abundance of midfielders used during that qualifying run. Due to injuries and players falling out of favour with the manager, Taylor gave caps to Dennis Wise (Wimbledon), Geoff Thomas (Crystal Palace), David Batty (Leeds) and Manchester United wonderkid Lee Sharpe. These players were not of the same calibre as Gazza, Platt and Robson, and they were hardly the players at the peak of the First Division.

More names would be put through the England selection machine with players such as Nigel Clough and Neil Webb filling holes in midfield. A whole host of players would be used as the season ploughed on and they finished 1991 with an invitational tournament in the southern hemisphere. Taylor had given debuts to 11 new faces in his first season in charge. The most damning statistics point to his legacy; those players earned a total of 130 caps, with 96 of those reserved for three players (Ian Wright, Wise and Batty).

It was becoming clear that English football had neither the quality in depth nor the right man for the job. English clubs' exclusion from European competition in the wake of the Heysel disaster had meant players were not exposed to the kind of football they were facing on the international stage. Obviously, there was nothing Taylor could do to change that, but maybe he had become a victim of that too.

The problems really started to gain pace in 1991/92. England stumbled towards the qualification finish line and after suffering his first defeat in charge to world champions Germany, two games remained for Taylor to secure England's place at the European Championships. Turkey at home and Poland away looked like winnable games, but positive performances were required to keep the fans on side.

England beat Turkey to put one foot in the finals, but it was neither a vintage, nor convincing performance. The Wembley crowd that had welcomed the players off the plane from Italy a year earlier were now booing. Taylor was interested in results and he knew that it was vital to get to the tournament. The scrutiny that greeted the result was a precursor for the vitriol that was about to come.

The game in Poland was tense. England were hardly firing on all cylinders in this early portion of Taylor's reign and the game in Poznań was no different. After falling behind in the first half, it was Gary Lineker who would make sure England's blushes were spared with a terrific second-half equaliser. Despite the unconvincing performance, Taylor had secured England's place at Euro 92.

In the build-up to the tournament, talk obviously turned to squad selection. Taylor had been hampered throughout qualifying by constant niggling injuries stopping Gazza from playing a major role. This is what, in part, led to so many changes in Taylor's line-up. Quality was still the issue and the selection dilemmas spread throughout the squad.

So, the time came for the squad to be announced. After using 51 players during his first two years in charge, Taylor was allowed to take 20 to Sweden. Despite having selected players like they were competition winners, the core of the side had been present at Italia 90. These players had been there in the pressure games and hopefully could do it again.

Every team needs a strong spine and Taylor had chosen the best one he had available. The likes of Woods, Pearce, Walker, Platt and Lineker were top players. Most teams in the tournament would have been happy to add any of them to their first XI. But one player who would not make the trip to the tournament was Gazza. After the horror injury he had suffered 12 months earlier, his further injury issues during recovery meant there was no way he would be able to play. This was a huge blow to Taylor but in truth, he had never been able to pick the best version of Gazza during his first two years in charge.

Added to the core were players who Taylor had given debuts to during his reign. Lee Dixon at right-back and Alan Smith were having great careers at Arsenal and only served to strengthen the side. Around the rest of the pitch, it was more difficult to see the direction he was taking. The use of so many players for three or four games made it hard to get any form of consistency in the squad or first-team selection. So, the rest of the squad was filled out with a huge number of inexperienced players at international level. Martin Keown, Keith Curle, Nigel Clough and Alan Shearer had barely made a dent for the national team. Between them they had earned just 17 caps. Those four were all good league players, but it was difficult to see what elite qualities they were going to bring to the team at that time. Keown and Curle were solid and Clough and Shearer had potential but did not seem like they were going to start or make a real name for themselves in the tournament.

For the most part, Taylor had his hand forced by who he had to pick. Injuries at right-back meant that he had to select Lee Dixon for the injured Rob Jones, but the fact that this choice was made despite Jones having only played one game speaks volumes for the selection process of the Taylor era. Dixon was selected ahead of Gary Stevens, who had been recalled briefly only to be dropped again.

Ian Wright was another to miss out. He was seen as a probable replacement for Lineker, but Taylor didn't believe the two could play together. So, he left Wright out of the squad. Selecting Shearer, who was not as established as Wright at that point, made that decision even more puzzling.

Chris Waddle had also fallen foul of Taylor. He had barely played under the new regime after being one of the most creative players under Robson and one of the best players in Europe. Excluding Waddle was made worse by the fact that John Barnes did not recover from a thigh strain in time for the tournament.

Clearly, injuries were playing a huge part in the lack of optimism around the team.

Taylor wasn't helped by injuries, but the way he dealt with some of his decisions left a sour taste in the mouth of some players. Two players, Gary Stevens and Mark Hateley, went public with their dismay at being omitted from the final 20-man squad. Both playing for Rangers north of the border, Stevens and Hateley were first-team regulars. Stevens was a solid right-back who looked set to take the place of the injured Lee Dixon. He had experienced disappointment from Bobby Robson too when he hadn't been selected for the World Cup squad two years earlier.

Hateley's position seemed more confusing. Alongside Ally McCoist, he played his part in one of the most prolific partnerships in Europe. He seemed like a perfect fit to play in a Graham Taylor side. The striker was not happy about the way Taylor had behaved either. All too frequently, the England boss had complained about players not notifying him of injuries or clubs holding them out of internationals, but a furious Hateley levelled the same criticism at Taylor for not informing him of the reasons behind his decision.

Understandably, Taylor had to pick the players he thought would fit his system and bring the most success. In truth, neither Stevens nor Hateley had been regulars. Leaving out Stevens proved to be a poor decision with England's lack of right-backs when the tournament started.

Added to the list of players staying at home was Gary Pallister. The tall defender was confident on the ball and would certainly have been at home against international opposition. In what was to become a sign of things to come for Pallister, the importance he had to his club was not mirrored on the international stage. For his skill on the ball alone, Pallister should have been an automatic choice in the squad.

Another player left at home was David Seaman. Now it seems like a very strange decision. A man who would go on to collect 75 caps for his country and perform in many tournaments was not always the first name on the team sheet. Seaman had played six times for Taylor up to that point but even his pedigree as a league winner with Arsenal was not enough to supplant Chris Woods in goal. In fairness to Woods, he had served his time behind Peter Shilton to step into the spotlight. What no one really expected was

Nigel Martyn being selected ahead of Seaman as the second-choice goalkeeper. Martyn had made one start under Taylor, but the manager felt he was ready to go to a tournament. It would prove to be one of the few times Martyn got ahead of Seaman in the international pecking order.

Now the squad was set, Taylor had to deal with the press who had mostly written England off before a ball was kicked. In the post-1992 years, the evaluation of England usually falls into one of two camps: this team is one of the best we have had in decades or this England team is the weakest we have fielded at a major tournament. Taylor's men certainly fell into the latter category.

England were drawn in Group A with France, Sweden and Yugoslavia. Having avoided Holland, Germany and Scotland for the group stage, Taylor was pleased. His record so far was strong, having only lost one game, and that was against the world champions. Clearly England had their issues, but on paper at least they were a hard team to beat.

Not only were they a hard team to beat, but England were also a hard team to watch. Three games were played in the tournament and just one goal scored. Two games finished 0-0 and in the third they were embarrassed by a vibrant Sweden team inspired by Tomas Brolin and Martin Dahlin. For Taylor it was an absolute disaster. All the troubles of injuries and selection headaches did not account for the fact that the performances were dismal. A solid, hard-to-beat side is all well and good, but this was not a league campaign played out over 40-plus games. International tournament games are few and they come quickly. If you haven't got that player or players to create something from nothing, progress is difficult.

The bad luck that spread through Taylor's defensive selections was bordering on farce. Dixon was injured and regained his fitness but was not selected. On the opposite side of things, Mark Wright was picked, but ended up aggravating an old Achilles injury on the eve of the tournament and had to withdraw. Disaster lurked at every turn for this team.

Failure in tournaments is nothing new to England. Whether it is freezing on the big stage or just not qualifying at all, Taylor's team were no different. Yes, there was bad luck, but decisions like taking off Gary Lineker against Sweden or selecting David Batty at right-back in the same game were baffling. Taylor was his own man, but he was clearly not the man for the job.

The next phase in his time as England manager would bring the nature of the role into question and make Taylor and his team a laughing stock. As this was the early 90s it had to involve television. Neil Duncanson, who will feature later with *Football Italia*, was a TV producer looking to create a series about the worst jobs in the world. After making a list of jobs, one particularly stood out: England manager. When no one was interested in creating a series, the company decided that, once Taylor had agreed, they would make a one-off programme. Having already produced a documentary about Gazza and his impending move to Lazio, Chrysalis Sport, despite no interest from TV broadcasters, were convinced that they could sell the project by the time it was finished so they decided to self-fund. It made sense: they could have total control and shape the project however they wanted.

Incredibly, the programme got the green light from everyone involved. After such a demoralising tournament, it would surely have made more sense for the FA to close shop and sort out what was going on with the team. Projects that remove focus from the core purpose never end well.

Football, as with all sports, has ups and downs on and off the pitch. Games can be dull, slow and uneventful. Training and media engagements can drag down players and managers too. But, *The Impossible Job*, as the documentary was now titled, showed all of that, warts and all. The access was just incredible. Never had people had the chance to see the inner workings (and failings) of a national team in this way. Most pieces on football were still promotional or smoothed over the cracks. Taylor certainly did not have that luxury.

What came from the documentary in terms of material was unprecedented. Players were shown having frank conversations with one another, Taylor and his assistants Phil Neal and Lawrie McMenemy looked perplexed, powerless, and confused about how to change things, and there were moments like David Platt being told he was losing the captaincy (which he had already been told before filming). The whole film, although an attempt to portray Taylor in a positive light, did nothing of the sort. It certainly cemented how he was not always in control of the job he was doing. Saying he was out of his depth is difficult because managing any football team is a challenge. Managing your home nation is a huge honour and the expectations after Italia 90 were enormous. A poor tournament in Sweden had quickly doused those flames of hope and the knives were being sharpened.

Events during the qualifying matches were bad enough but seeing them through the eyes of television cameras just made things even bleaker. There was no way that Taylor was going to be able to stay in the job considering there would be no World Cup for England. His performance in front of the cameras was the last straw.

There are numerous famous games during that qualifying campaign. If you mention Oslo, Rotterdam and Bologna to certain England fans they will instantly remember iconic images of Taylor. Against Egil Olsen's Norway, the England boss's shouts of 'Hit Les' as England stumbled to an awful 2-0 defeat still live on. Ronald Koeman was public enemy number one after his performance for Holland in Rotterdam. He orchestrated a 2-0 defeat of England thanks to yanking down David Platt and staying on the pitch, followed by the ultimate villain move of scoring a free kick in the second half. And in Bologna, well, San Marino scored after nine seconds. The final score was 7-1 to England, but they needed to win by seven clear goals to have a chance of qualifying for USA 94. The impossible job had become a disaster.

Despite all of that, Taylor remained friendly with the director Ken McGill and even stood by his decision to appear on the documentary. An honest man to the last, Taylor knew that showing himself warts and all was a gamble. He took the risk and it backfired. If England had qualified maybe it would have been a different story. The truth was that it was a huge misjudgement on his part.

Before long Taylor was out of a job. The press-anointed 'Turnip Taylor' was to be replaced with a manager much more used to constant attention: Terry Venables. The ex-Barcelona and Spurs manager was an inspired choice by the Football Association. Whatever the reservations around Venables's off-field interests (of which there were many), he was a first-class manager with a CV featuring many top clubs. He was more approachable with the media and the often-defensive nature of Taylor's interactions was gone. The other benefit he had was that England would not have to qualify for the next tournament – Euro 96 – as they were hosting it.

To add to the cards in Venables's favour, the group of players that emerged as the Premier League took hold of domestic football was far superior to those available to Taylor. Some of the old faces were quickly discarded and replaced with potential stars.

A new wave of music, Britpop, was sweeping the country and football was quick to latch on to its coat-tails. Going to matches was cool. Watching football was cool again. *Fever Pitch* had changed a lot of opinions about the matchday fan and who they were. The days of the football hooligan were disappearing. That vision of a middle-class audience was being realised. For better or worse, the gentrification of football was on the horizon, but the Venables reign and Euro 96 certainly felt like the high point of an era.

Press attention in the two years of friendlies that led up to the first major tournament on home soil since 1966 focused on the hangover from the Taylor era and Venables's struggle to get Shearer scoring. As had been the case with his predecessor, games were low-scoring and there was no sign of any real attacking flair in the side. The fact that the games were non-competitive, with nothing but pride at stake, made it difficult to feel any sense of urgency or jeopardy.

Taylor may have been criticised when he was given the England job for his lack of experience in European competitions for example, but his integrity was not called into question in the same way as Venables's. The new England boss was mentioned in Parliament multiple times by MP Kate Hoey over some of his transfer dealings. An investigation by the Premier League into the transfer of Teddy Sheringham to Spurs from Nottingham Forest had taken two years and was yet to reach a verdict. It wasn't all 'Football's Coming Home' during his reign.

Although Venables was being scrutinised off the pitch, the England players on it were of a different calibre to the ones Taylor had to choose from. Of course, there were some players who lasted even from the Italia 90 squad, but Venables was able to call upon a new crop of younger players who were excelling as their teams competed in the Premier League.

This created the crescendo that was Euro 96. The fever that swept through England at this point was a huge catalyst in the growth of the Premier League. It also created great swathes of support for Terry

Venables, despite, due to ongoing court proceedings, the manager saying he would step down once the tournament had been completed. Like Bobby Robson before him, Venables knew the tournament was his last hurrah.

The opener against Switzerland felt like it was from the Taylor archives, albeit the 1-1 draw put an end to the Shearer goal drought. Beating Scotland thanks to a Seaman penalty save and a Gazza wonder-goal was huge. The nation was behind the team. After disastrous performances under Taylor and two years of friendlies, fans believed that England as a team were back on the map and back in their hearts. Football fever swept the nation.

Peaking against Holland, Venables's side demolished what was a superb group of players. The Dutch had no answer to England, who were ruthless. Shearer would break the world transfer record in a matter of weeks and it showed with his performance.

Clearly, the real shame was that England again found themselves knocked out in the semi-final on penalties against Germany. Football very nearly came home, but the highs of that tournament meant

England were in a very different place to Taylor's side in 1992.

Glenn Hoddle followed Venables into the hot seat and took his talented side to France for the World Cup, only to be undone on penalties again. He was tactically astute, had built a strong group of players and knew what he wanted to achieve. He also had the chance to blood even more young players who would dominate the domestic game.

As with Venables, off-field circumstances meant that Hoddle would not be a long-term manager for England. Comments he made linked to his beliefs ensured that Hoddle was quickly shown the door before the campaign for Euro 2000 was in full flow.

The next few years for England included the abortive reign of Kevin Keegan. A man who many thought would bring a swashbuckling style to the national team instead brought confusion and elimination. By his own frank admission, Keegan was not cut out for the job and resigned after a rain-soaked Wembley defeat to Germany.

The press had a field day with England's next manager, who had the greatest generation of players the nation had ever seen. Sven-Göran Eriksson was a hugely successful coach on the continent and was England's first foreign manager. He almost guaranteed qualification to major tournaments and a place in the last 16. The problems came when the journalists hounded him and anyone he was involved with for a salacious story. Media was changing and the age of constant scrutiny was here. It was a far cry from the days of 'Taylor the Turnip', but 'Sven the Swede' was the successor. Constant coverage of his private life, which provided many column inches, certainly got in the way of the work he did with the team. Should they have achieved more? Yes, but Eriksson was a success. Trying to bring him down was the natural thing to do in the eyes of the media. Build them up to knock them down.

The challenges faced by an England boss are clear. The weight of expectation to deliver a tournament win is huge. Because the Premier League is the biggest league in the world, it seems logical that the national team will share the same dominance. That is certainly not the case, thanks to the volume of players from overseas in the league in the last 20-plus years. More recently, time and money has been given to youth and academy development and England now have a strong crop of players in several age groups.

Dealing with and managing expectations is another occupational hazard. The press have long made the England boss a target for their column inches. What was served up to Taylor was vitriolic and symptomatic of a media that was becoming more invasive during a decade of huge growth in television coverage of football. He remained dignified throughout, even if his team never quite made the impact he wanted.

4

Europe in Flux:
Danish Dynamite reborn

IT IS 1986. The World Cup in Mexico. A tournament of colour, extreme heat, and some incredible footballers. Diego Maradona and his Argentina side may have stolen all of the headlines, but one team stole people's hearts: Denmark.

Playing in an incredible Hummel-designed, half-and-half red and white pin-striped patterned kit that had to be seen to be enjoyed, the innovative shirt design matched the supreme talent and skill on show from a team that had qualified for its first World Cup. Players like Michael Laudrup, Morten Olsen, Soren Lerby, Preben Elkjær and Frank Arnesen wowed crowds with their possession-based football in a system that prioritised astute movement and tactical awareness. They were also blessed with goals.

Thrashing Uruguay 6-1 in the group stages was the clear high point. They were a team built to thrill with players that had the confidence and technical ability to compete on any stage. The understanding between each member of the team was crucial. Flexibility across the squad meant that players were confident attacking from anywhere on the pitch.

Elkjær and Laudrup were superb. Already playing in Serie A, Laudrup was just 21 years old when he started the tournament. He formed a superb partnership up front with Elkjær, who also played in Italy. His goals had led Hellas Verona to their first ever league title and he had finished in the top three of the *Ballon d'Or* in 1984 and 85. These two players were reaching the top of their game and added the dynamite to this Danish side.

Just ten years before Mexico, Denmark had still been adapting to a fully professional national team after decades as solely amateurs. Similarly, the Danish leagues only allowed for amateurs, so the players that wanted to become professional had to cast their eye further afield. A huge benefit for the national team during the 80s, the fact that so many of their squad had experience of many different playing styles meant they were quickly able to form a coherent unit because of their inherent adaptability.

Once the Danish Football Union (DBU) realised that to build a team worthy of competing in the best international tournaments they needed to change, the slow building process reached its peak in 1986, after an attempt to qualify for the World Cup in 1982 had been ultimately unsuccessful. However, the team did experience their first moment in the professional limelight with a run to the semi-finals of the 1984 European Championships before defeat against Spain ended the dream.

That 1986 team will live long in the memory of football fans thanks to their superb football and captivating image.

Attacking football always brings spectators to their feet and having a team do it on a stage like the World Cup cements your legacy as a player and team.

Immediately after World War I, in 1918, the Kingdom of Serbs, Croats and Slovenes emerged from the division of Austria-Hungary. The Kingdom of Yugoslavia was then formed in 1929 after King Alexander I took charge. Quickly, a football team for Yugoslavia was created, ready to compete in the first ever World Cup, held in Uruguay. Thirteen teams took part in that first tournament, with Yugoslavia being one of only two from Europe. They emerged with two wins from their group alongside Brazil and Bolivia, before being defeated 6-1 by eventual winners Uruguay in the semi-final.

Controversially, the team consisted solely of players based at Serbian football clubs. Because the football association headquarters had been moved from Zagreb to Belgrade, many of the national team regulars of Croatian descent were not selected. The political and footballing difficulties persisted between the two nations with the formation of independent Croatian teams in the 1940s.

The 1960s proved to be the most successful for the Yugoslavian team with runners-up finishes in the European Championships of 1960 and 68, plus another fourth-place World Cup finish in 1962. They had already added the Olympic title in 1960 and were fast developing a reputation as a skilful and attacking team. Like that Danish side of 1986.

Skipping forward to the 1980s, the death of President Tito brought turmoil to the structure of Yugoslavia for the decade. The fall of the Soviet Union had a massive impact on the nations within Yugoslavia, added to the uncertainty and, along with the arrival of Slobodan Milošević, increased the pace of collapse.

However, in football terms, the 1980s was about to bless Yugoslavia with its very own golden generation of players. Every nation seems to have them and if the stars align then success grows ever closer. For Yugoslavia, the Under-21 World Cup in 1987 showed the world that a talented group of players was emerging in the south-east of Europe. Defeating a strong German side managed by Berti Vogts and featuring Andreas Möller, the pieces were in place.

Looking back at the names of players from youth tournaments can be a roll-call of wasted talent or unfulfilled potential. The difficulty in transitioning from a player in junior football to senior football is huge. Numerous elements need to line up for players to be a success. Even then, managers and coaches need to believe in you and see how you can fit into their side. In the case of this Yugoslavian team, there was no danger of their star players missing out on the big time.

The players that led the side in 1987 bring up instant memories of their contribution to football; Robert Jarni, Zvonimir Boban, Davor Šuker, Igor Štimac, Robert Prosinečki and Predrag Mijatovič. These players would go on to have incredible careers for their clubs and even win European Cups and Champions Leagues. They were a group of players that were so talented they were attracting the attention of clubs across Europe already. The stage was set for them to arrive on football's biggest stage at Italia 90.

To explain the sheer wealth of talent in Yugoslavia at the time, Siniša Mihajlovic, Vladimir Jugovic and Alen Bokšić were all told that they would be left at home to gain more experience. Clearly, there was strength in depth in teams across the nation and it was only a matter of time before they would be challenging at the top of the world game.

Added to the youngsters was a core of players that already featured in Europe's biggest leagues. Throw in players from the Partizan and Red Star of Belgrade, others from Dinamo Zagreb and you have a very competitive squad. The likes of Darko Pančev and Dejan Savićević were other young talents breaking through at home, with big moves on the horizon.

The player that knitted the team together and showed truly world-class ability was Dragan Stojković. A classic number ten, his technique was exemplary and the way he played was a joy, balancing his role between midfield and forward positions. An inventive and elegant dribbler, he was on the wanted list of many European clubs with Milan and Juventus chasing him, before Marseille won the battle, spending £5.5m to sign him after Italia 90.

One player that would miss the finals was Boban. As difficulties mounted in Yugoslavia, the dissent spilled over on to the football pitch. Tensions between Serbs and Croats were reaching their peak as the referendum on independence loomed. Boban found himself in the middle of it. A proud Croat, Boban was the best player in the country and an idol for Dinamo Zagreb. So, when they faced off against rivals Red Star Belgrade, inevitably trouble occurred. Mere months before Boban would have been taking his place in the Yugoslavia squad for a summer of World Cup football, he was banned for six months for kicking a police officer. He was captain and leader of Dinamo. The player the fans looked up to. When he thought he saw the fans being mistreated by the police (who were all Serbs, despite the game being played in Zagreb), he intervened and kicked the officer. The Red Star players had left the pitch, quickly finding their way to the dressing room. Boban's standing amongst the Dinamo fans became clear. A human shield was erected around him by the Bad Blue Boys, Dinamo's fans. Immediately Boban became a national hero to Croats and was identified as a Croat nationalist in Serbia.

Punishment was swift and severe. Boban was suspended by the Football Association of Yugoslavia for six months and had criminal charges filed against him. The riot was one of the key moments in the end of the Yugoslav First League, with independence not far away. Italia 90 had been robbed of a player that was on the verge of stardom and two republics had served to widen the divide between them.

Denmark did not qualify for the World Cup in 1990. They finished behind Romania in the qualification group stage and were the lowest-ranked runner-up so did not make the finals. It marked the end of Sepp Piontek's tenure as Denmark's manager. He had transformed the team and made them relevant on the European stage. Long-time number two Richard Møller Nielsen was the man who replaced him after Horst Wohlers was not allowed to be released from his contract with Bayer Uerdingen.

The first problems that Nielsen encountered were with his star men, Michael and Brian Laudrup. Both quit the national team after three games of the qualifying campaign for Euro 92. Jan Mølby was another who joined the brothers in quitting the team. This was not ideal during a difficult qualification campaign that would see Nielsen's men in a group alongside Yugoslavia.

Michael Laudrup did not mince his words when it came to Nielsen's approach. The star of the side said, 'We aren't the European Brazilians anymore. Now we are more like the Swedes, basing our soccer on physical strength rather than fantasy.' The lack of flair was a crucial component missing from what was a defensive and functional team. It would only continue in that vein with the loss of the Laudrups.

Denmark had troubles, but Yugoslavia were the best team in the group. They won their first three games, scoring eight goals in the process, and capped off 1990 with a 2-0 win against Denmark. Darko Pančev was the standout performer, as he would be for Red Star Belgrade, who were about to take over European football.

Red Star had never won a European tournament. The club, rich with a diverse, multi-ethnic squad that reflected the country, had come close on multiple occasions, but never managed to get into the final. When they did get to the UEFA Cup Final in 1979, they lost in a tight contest against Borussia Mönchengladbach. It would be over a decade later that they would get a chance to add a European trophy to the endless stream of league titles.

The 1990/91 season felt like it was the right time for Red Star to win it. The triumph in 1987, the performances of Italia 90 and the turmoil at home meant lifting the European Cup could be a transcendent moment.

It helped that their side was full of brilliant players. Having Savićević, Prosinećki and Pančev as the three most important players in the side meant they were like the great Italian sides who had a trio of stars to lead them to glory.

One player who would not take the pitch for Red Star that season was Stojković, who had left for Marseille. Tragically, he suffered a serious knee injury, which meant he missed a huge part of the 1990/91 season. Ironically, as his new team progressed through the rounds of the European Cup, it became clear that Red Star would be the team to stand in the way of their triumph.

Qualification for the final was relatively straightforward for Red Star until the semi-final against Bayern Munich, when they needed an injury-time own goal to secure passage to the final in Bari, where they would face Marseille. There, they were shut off from distractions. Numerous European clubs were already trying to break up the talented young group of players, so their focus had to be on the game.

In contrast to the swashbuckling style of previous rounds, and the attitude of the national team, Red Star took a different approach to the final. Emulating Steaua Bucharest, the first ever Eastern European winner of the trophy, they played for penalties. Sometimes, performances don't matter in a final, it is the winning that counts. Red Star manager Ljupko Petrović believed there was no other way that his team could contain the immense Marseille front line: Chris Waddle, Abedi Pele and Jean-Pierre Papin. He might have been wrong, but he didn't care about that as he lifted the trophy.

The stark reality for this Red Star side was that all the European Cup-winning team had gone a year later. A country that was no longer safe had lost its finest generation of players.

Continuing on the pitch, the qualification campaign for Euro 92 remained tight. In May 91, Denmark beat Yugoslavia in Belgrade. Both countries were making easy work of the other teams in the group, and it looked like one more slip-up would mean that Yugoslavia would be knocked off their perch. Denmark, still without the Laudrups, continued in the hope they could earn a spot as a runner-up.

Politically, things had changed drastically in Yugoslavia by the summer of 1991. Croatia and Slovenia declared themselves independent, after referendums showed public support for breaking away. Milošević did not recognise the results and began military action. The dissolution of Yugoslavia had begun.

Politics and football often mix; players get dragged in too. Prosinećki was the target of venomous abuse and threats thanks to reports in Yugoslavia that said he was the son of a Serb and a Croat. Real Madrid were reluctant to let him report for international duty with death threats out against him. Prosinećki told fans that he was a committed Yugoslav and would be there for his team. Ultimately, it didn't work out that way. Two weeks before the match against the Faroe Islands, Prosinećki pulled out of the squad, injured and unfit to play.

Football continued and by the end of 1991, Yugoslavia were still out in front against Denmark and had qualified for the finals of Euro 92 in Sweden, a huge achievement despite the tensions. There were of course factions within the team in terms of which republic players were from, but as a group they all represented Yugoslavia.

A prerequisite for any team to enter a FIFA-approved competition is United Nations acceptance that a nation has political independence. At the point of qualification, Yugoslavia still maintained this right. How long this would last was another matter. FIFA and UEFA kept track of the ever-developing situation; with all Croatian players now excluded from playing for the national side, there was potential for tensions to escalate further. In January 1992, Lennart Johansson, president of UEFA, asked Denmark to act as stand-by for the tournament in case the civil war escalated in Yugoslavia to the point they would not be able to take part.

Once the draw was made in Gothenburg, both Yugoslavia and CIS (Commonwealth of Independent States) were given until 1 April to confirm their places in the finals. CIS was created after the fall of the Soviet Union, but Latvia, Estonia and Lithuania were independent states and within FIFA in that guise. Ukraine were happy for their players to take part in the tournament, knowing that they would probably gain full FIFA membership after the Euro 92 tournament was over. There was no end to the complications of the evolution of Eastern Europe.

In Group One with Yugoslavia were England, France, and hosts Sweden. None of those teams possessed the level of technical ability the Yugoslavia side could put out. Graham Taylor's England had made hard work of a straightforward qualifying group, Sweden were an unknown quantity and France had steamrollered all-comers on the way to the finals. On paper, Yugoslavia looked at least as strong as France. If they had been able to select their Croatian stars, then they would probably have been favourites for the tournament.

Denmark and Nielsen had to lick their wounds but stay ready. They had missed out on another major tournament, albeit by a fine margin. Better results earlier in the qualification stage may have resulted in a different outcome. Pressure from managing without their two main stars was not easy either.

Having been robbed of several established players, Yugoslavia manager Ivica Osim had a difficult task ahead of him. He had no idea when he would have any foreign-based players to work with and the domestic championship did not end until 24 May. Not ideal when he was preparing a team to compete against some of Europe's best. During the months leading up to the tournament, Osim's position had become more and more difficult. Football was not dictating his job anymore. Political upheaval and violence were at the forefront of the manager's mind. As a Bosnian, he knew that his family and home could be caught up in a war that seemed inevitable.

Throughout the first few months of 1992, Osim considered his position. He was approached about the Israel job, and had offers from Bayern Munich, clubs in Qatar and one from a club in Denmark. There were threats from other republics within Yugoslavia to withdraw players from his squad and further weaken it. Even with numerous players unavailable, if he intended to stay in charge, Osim had a fine group of players to choose from. There was no Boban, Jarni or Prosinečki but there was Savićević, Mihajlovic and Pančev. Each player could be a match-winner and if they could field a team, the semi-finals were not out of reach.

All the promotional materials from magazines to book and newspaper previews, still featured segments on the brilliance of the Red Star players and their potential to spring an upset against the more established powers. Some of those previews and analysts commented on the desperate situation and most wanted Yugoslavia kicked out and replaced with Denmark.

Decision time arrived for UEFA. There was only one thing they could do. War was raging through Yugoslavia, with a conflict in Bosnia beginning in April 1992. Games were no longer allowed to be staged in Belgrade, so Red Star faced Sampdoria in Sofia in the European Cup and were unable to progress to the final and defend their crown. Time was ticking towards the final decision on Yugoslavia's plight.

In the days leading up to the tournament, announcements surfaced one by one. The first, on 29 May 1992, was from Lennart Johansson who stated that Yugoslavia would be able to compete at Euro 92, pending the outcome of the United Nations sanctions. A day later, the UN sanctioned Yugoslavia, including a ban on all sporting links. FIFA then announced that Yugoslavia were suspended from international football. UEFA completed the round with the invitation to Denmark to compete in Sweden.

The Danes, who were about to enjoy their holidays, accepted the invitation and would take up the eighth and final place at the tournament. It was an incredible turnaround for Nielsen, who had a lot of work to do to gain the confidence of his players and hope to put out a competitive side. One benefit to his team qualifying was the return of Brian Laudrup, who had agreed to withdraw his resignation from the team.

Just prior to the decisions, Ivica Osim resigned from his position as Yugoslavia national team manager.

The final straw had come when his hometown of Sarajevo was attacked during the early days of the Bosnian War. He quickly found a new team in Panathinaikos. Yugoslavia were confident enough at this point to appoint a manager for the tournament; legendary figure Miljan Miljanić. It was to no avail as their suspension came within days.

Denmark assembled their squad and headed for neighbouring Sweden. The group was full of experience. Most of them were domestic-based, but the two stars played in two of Europe's top leagues: goalkeeper Peter Schmeichel and forward Brian Laudrup. Schmeichel had elevated his game at Manchester United and was getting a reputation as one of the best goalkeepers in the league and Europe. Laudrup had been playing well for Bayern Munich before injuries had hampered his progress.

Taking Yugoslavia's place gave Denmark matches against England, Sweden and then France. They had nothing to fear, and they certainly weren't there to make up the numbers. Nielsen and his players had a chance to prove that they should be there. In the first game of the group against England, they more than matched Taylor's team. England were mired in injury problems, selection issues and a lack of real playing identity, so did not prove to be too much of a threat. Denmark had struggled to find their feet in the first half but dominated the second with John Jensen the most influential player in midfield, dictating the play and coming close to scoring.

Up next were hosts Sweden, who attacked Denmark for the whole game. They were good value for the win, with up-and-coming star Tomas Brolin the man to win the game for the hosts. Both sides had chances, Schmeichel made some good saves, and the home side were powered on by a rapturous partisan crowd. Despite the defeat, Denmark showed potential. France, who had been one of the favourites, had recorded two draws including a drab 0-0 affair against England. A win against France, and Denmark would be into the semi-finals.

Henrik Larsen was the early hero in the final group game. He was a replacement in the starting line-up for Kim Vilfort, who temporarily left the tournament to look after his daughter who was being treated for leukaemia. Larsen's goal set up the victory and despite Papin getting Platini's side back into it, the Danes answered with an inspired substitution from

Nielsen. Once Laudrup started to tire, Lars Elstrup was brought on and he changed the game. Denmark ended up with a 2-1 win and a second-place finish in the group. The incredible story would continue in the semi-finals.

In Group Two, the Netherlands recorded wins against Germany and Scotland, with a 0-0 draw against CIS rounding off their results. They looked fluent and confident. Dennis Bergkamp, Marco Van Basten and Ruud Gullit were quality players that defences could not deal with. Add to that players like Ronald Koeman and Frank Rijkaard and you can see why many tipped the Dutch to go far. They would face Denmark in the semi-final.

The Netherlands were favourites. Not just for this game, but for the whole tournament. Rinus Michels in the dugout knew he had a group of incredibly talented players. However, tournaments are not always about talent, but about teamwork, effort and drive. Denmark showed they had that in spades. No way had they come this far to go down without a fight.

Back for the semi-final was Vilfort, who was now travelling home between games to be with his daughter. A truly incredible story. The midfielder was a key component of the Danish side and his presence galvanised the team.

Not content with showing the Dutch their team spirit, Denmark could play too. Larsen found the net again, within five minutes this time after great work from Brian Laudrup, whose performance would only be topped by the heroics of Schmeichel. The Dutch were shell-shocked. This was not in the script.

After Bergkamp equalised with a shot that skidded through Schmeichel, another goal from Larsen meant the Danes led 2-1 going into the last five minutes of the game. Always a dangerous time, they finally succumbed to Dutch pressure, Rijkaard finding the back of the net and ultimately sending the game to a penalty shoot-out after a goalless extra period. Never an enjoyable way to decide a match, this could have been a cruel way to end the Danish fairy tale.

Both teams scored with their first penalties. The ever-reliable Koeman fired his shot into the roof of the net and the man of the moment Larsen squeezed his penalty past Van Breukelen. Next up, Marco Van Basten. At the time, he was the best striker in Europe playing for the best club side and one of the strongest national teams. He was, however, about to take a penalty in the semi-final of a European Championship. Anything could happen and it did. Schmeichel matched Van Basten and saved the spot kick. The great Dane let out a huge roar and pumped his fist to the crowd. This was his moment. Van Basten could only puff out his cheeks and return to his team-mates.

Everyone else had scored their penalties. Denmark would now have a shot to win it. Kim Christofte of Brøndby stepped up with the weight of a nation on his shoulders. It was hard to tell from the way he strolled up to the ball, cool and calm, getting enough power on it to roll it into the net. Van Breukelen went the other way, a look of resignation on his face as the ball went past him.

Christofte spun on the penalty spot, his arms aloft. The moment was huge. Schmeichel charged over to the big defender, lifted him up and ran in sheer joy. Denmark had made it to the final. A team that entered the tournament just over three weeks earlier had now made it all the way.

Players and fans celebrated together. This was a team in unison, built on a spirit that kept them together. The exclusion of players in the past was long forgotten, because it was this group of hard-working and effective players that had executed a plan perfectly. Now they had a chance to win it all against a Germany side that had eliminated hosts Sweden the day before.

Denmark went one better in the final. Their resolve and endeavour was more than enough to beat a German team that could not break down Denmark's defence or resolve. No matter how they pushed, Nielsen's side did not break. Goals from Jensen and the incredible Vilfort won it for the Danes in 90 minutes. From nowhere, Denmark emerged as a bastion of hope for teams everywhere. A group of players who were given no hope had done the unthinkable.

The closer the match got to its conclusion the more Denmark could sense a win. So, they exploited the rules as much as possible to whittle down the time. The back-pass rule was still unchanged at this point, despite being on the cards since the end of Italia 90. Germany v Denmark in the Euro 92 final was the final nail in its coffin. Frustrating Germany by simply going back to Schmeichel as much as possible, Denmark stopped the flow of the game and more importantly kept hold of the ball. The spectacle slowly drained from the game, but Denmark did not care. They were going to be champions. Most players would do anything to get a victory of that magnitude in their careers and Denmark did just that. Winning was the only option.

Special mention must also go to Kim Vilfort for his superhuman mental strength. The midfielder had real doubts about whether he should return to the tournament after visiting his stricken daughter. Her health improved during his visit and Vilfort's wife implored her husband to re-join his team-mates. He didn't know what to do until his four-year-old son asked him why he wasn't playing. Vilfort travelled back to Sweden to play his part in an historic event.

In truth, the underdog story is part of the fabric of sport. Denmark truly were one of the great underdogs and proved that anything is possible. As football moved towards a monopoly at the top of the game, their victory in 1992 is a blot on the competition record, like Greece in 2004 and Leicester in 2016. People will look back and think, how did that happen?

For Yugoslavia, years of conflict would grip the country. Football became a minor consideration when people were dying for their beliefs. The wars continued to rage through the 1990s with the dissolution of Yugoslavia coming in 1992. From this, the Federal Republic of Yugoslavia (FRY) rose in the republics of Serbia and Montenegro while war continued in Croatia and Bosnia.

Within weeks of the final whistle blowing at Euro 92, Croatia were readmitted into FIFA. Although unable to take part in the qualifying campaign for the World Cup in the United States in 1994, Croatia did enter qualification for Euro 96. A chance for players to play in a tournament they had been banned from, and their original home nation had been expelled from.

That Croatian side from Euro 96 is remembered by many. Incredibly, they were drawn with Denmark in the group stage. Of course, there had to be an iconic moment in that game, and it came from Davor Šuker, who was audacious enough to lob Peter Schmeichel in the final minute of a game Croatia went on to win 3-0. Not content with beating the holders, they ran Germany close in the knockout round, before falling to a 2-1 defeat.

Both Croatia and the FRY qualified for the 1998 World Cup in France and made it out of the group stages. Croatia were a revelation. They built on the success they had two years earlier and made it to the semi-finals against eventual winners France. Losing 2-1 to a home side buoyed by a huge crowd in Paris was an incredible achievement for a country formed six years earlier, and testament to the brilliance of those players who stood up for what they believed in and were able to represent their country at the highest level.

In the case of the FRY, there were a lot of familiar faces from the late 80s who were tipped to make it on the big stage. Real Madrid's Predrag Mijatović was a star, Mihajlović, Jugović and Savićević all played in Serie A, while the player who was thought to be the best of them all was now 33 and featuring in the J-League for Nagoya Grampus Eight, Dragan Stojković. Finally, these players had been able to show their skills at the World Cup again after their prime years on the international stage were taken away.

Progress for the Federal Republic of Yugoslavia was stopped by the Netherlands. Dennis Bergkamp scored just as he had done against their replacements in Euro 92. In four tournament games, FRY played two opponents that Denmark had faced on their way to European glory. Fate maybe, or just another random act in the world of football.

Denmark have never been able to match their victory at Euro 92, becoming a solid international side that has qualified for tournaments, threatened to do well, but never quite delivered. Quality players are still brought through in a nation with a tiny population compared to the other superpowers of Europe. The victory in 1992 will forever be remembered in world football and the way in which it came about through conflict in Yugoslavia changed the geographical landscape of the game. More teams, more players and bigger tournaments were to follow as FIFA expanded with the break-up of the Soviet Union and the independence of smaller nations.

5

Can He Kick It?
Keepers on the ball

IBROX, 30 September 1987. Rangers v Dynamo Kiev in round one of the European Cup. The Scottish champions are about to progress into the next round. They are 2-0 up thanks to goals from Mark Falco and Ally McCoist.

All they need to do is keep the ball and see off any disasters. Enter Graeme Souness.

Receiving the ball in the middle of Kiev's half, Souness turns. He's facing his own goal. The huge number six on his back is now facing the opponents' goal. He digs his foot deep under the ball and lofts an enormous clearance high into the air. Floating far above all the defenders, it closes in on Chris Woods's goal. One bounce and the ball drops into the keeper's arms. Possession secured again; time successfully wasted.

Now, this is an extreme example of keeping the ball at all costs. It is not necessarily a typical example of playing the back pass either. But, it was within the rules of the game. Looking back, with the current modern penchant for sweeper keepers and the player between the sticks being an extra ball-player, the sight is odd to say the least.

Souness knew that he had this in his locker. He was an excellent passer and could make the distance, even if the ball only just dropped where it needed to. Any shorter and the attacker was in on goal. Using the back pass as a tactic to keep the ball was commonplace, so despite the way it looks today, in 1987 it was a great tactical play.

Whether it was the most aesthetic way to play the game is another matter.

Football had come to a crossroads in the early 1990s. The previous decade had not had the same verve and vitality of the 1970s, with its virtuoso players. For the 80s, the off-field problems that hampered the game's growth were compounded by a lack of quality on it. On the whole, a more mechanical and system-based approach to tactics meant the game was starting to look different.

In the past, football had not prioritised innovation. Tweaks and adaptations had been made over time, like the introduction of additional substitutes, extra time and penalty shoot-outs, but the game had stayed true to its origins for a large portion of history. Managers and players were the changing parts of the game, perfecting new formations, techniques, and positions to defeat their opponents.

FIFA knew they needed to make changes after their comprehensive post-World Cup report on Italia 90. A tournament that had captured the imagination of English fans thanks to last-minute goals and the rise of Gazza, did not produce football of any level of excitement. Football was being consumed by more and more people on television and if the product was not engaging enough then entertainment would be sought elsewhere. Football was now fighting in a crowded marketplace.

The report outlined that the final itself had been 'a dreadful advertisement for the game of football'. A game that should have showcased the biggest sport in the world had become mired in cards, a lack of quality and diving. Time-wasting was another red flag for FIFA, who commented on this in earlier games in the tournament.

New stadia and the incredible atmosphere at matches across the tournament had been an unmitigated success. Memories of Roger Milla, Carlos Valderrama and the like will forever be etched into the memories of a whole generation of fans. Still, the product on the pitch had to be right, so FIFA got to the drawing board and, with the help of a wide-ranging cast of experts, set about changing the rules to make the game faster with goals at the forefront.

The first inkling of a change to the back-pass law came from an unlikely source; Daniel Jeandupeux. The Caen manager sent a letter to FIFA in December 1990, which outlined ways in which the laws of the game could reduce time-wasting. Jeandupeux's ideas were well received by FIFA's general secretary Sepp Blatter, who wanted to improve the game after seeing some of the tactics employed by teams a few months earlier at the World Cup.

Details of the letter were shared with *The Athletic* by Jeandupeux. He had researched how long his own goalkeeper had held the ball. Shocked by what he found, he noted that the stats made him believe that this behaviour was 'incompatible with the spectacular/remarkable side of football'. Like FIFA, Jeandupeux wanted to come up with an idea that would keep the speed of the game that so excited fans. Changing the current rule to something more progressive was his first thought. In his letter he outlined how goalkeepers should have only three seconds to release the ball and he should not be allowed to pick the ball up after receiving it from a team-mate. Punishment would be a free kick to the attacking side.

Interestingly, he had also noted that the ball had gone out of play 85 times in the game between Caen and Sochaux. Every throw-in was estimated to take between 10 and 17 seconds, so an awful lot of game time was eroded by this one simple action. This led to another proposed rule, which did not get the same attention, but has more recently been used to full effect in the modern game; a multiball system.

Right there in his letter is the idea to have seven or eight balls around the pitch to reduce the time needed to get the ball back into play. 1992 is over

30 years ago now, but who said those times weren't progressive too?

Once the letter reached Blatter and his football task force, wheels were set in motion to bring a rule change to the IFAB (International Football Association Board), preventing goalkeepers from handling back passes. At the board meeting, Blatter and the group requested a trial to be carried out at the 1991 Under-17 World Championship. Permission was granted and the new rule would be trialled in the tournament, held in Italy, of course.

Reaction to the proposed rule changes was, as to be expected, divided. Writing in *World Soccer*, Keir Radnedge believed that this new rule would simply overcomplicate the game. Football was simple, he wrote, and anything that jeopardises that will remove all its beauty and strength. He turned to the players themselves and suggested that most defenders would balloon the ball into the crowd rather than being able to pass it more safely to the goalkeeper.

In the next edition of the magazine, Brian Glanville chimed in with his opinions. Not one to shy away from saying exactly what he thought, the writer said the cheap gimmick would prevent more goals being scored. Glanville was much more content with leaving the back pass exactly as it was, 'a potential bore, but also a rich source of human error'.

Strength in simplicity was the message from Radnedge and Glanville, who most certainly saw this meddling from the administrators as detrimental to a game that had lasted so long in its current form. Taking the message more broadly, it was clear that the influence of external forces was starting to take hold of the game. As with most of the innovations in 1992, exposure of the 'product' was key as that is what brought in the revenue.

The trial at the Under-17 World Championship was considered a success and so the rule was ready for a professional trial. In the same tournament a strange change to the offside rule, which allowed a player to stand on the edge of the opposition's box without punishment, was tried but failed miserably and was quickly swept away. FIFA ensured that the back-pass rule could be put into place quickly, after initially proposing its use in the World Cup in 1994.

Another nail in the coffin for the old rules was the performance of Denmark in the final of the European Championships in 1992. Blatter and his team must have felt vindicated watching Peter Schmeichel exchange endless passes with his defenders. The triumphant story of Denmark was incredible, but underneath the surface it was another low-scoring affair. More so than ever, the new rule needed to come into force. As time dwindled on the clock in the final, the last ever legal back pass to be handled by a goalkeeper was from German defender Stefan Reuter to Bodo Illgner.

In that same summer another football tournament would take place, at the Olympic Games in Barcelona. The men's football tournament would be the first official competition to adopt the new rule, with the hope all FIFA competitions would be ready to roll it out in the 1992/93 season. Luckily, there were no other proposals to contend with, so it was left to the players to see how the new rule worked.

Around this time the FIFA Football 2000 commission was set up to create new changes to the game. After a year of work, they suggested sending off players who tried to score with a deliberate handball, increasing the number of balls around the pitch (as suggested by Daniel Jeandupeux), using a sin bin, scrapping penalty shoot-outs and more. Michel

Platini suggested that the proposals could go further and introduce the use of television replays to decide contentious incidents. Who said VAR was just a modern invention?

Sepp Blatter was confident that the rule change they had selected to bring in worldwide was the right one. He believed that the move would reduce the amount of time-wasting and increase the amount of time the ball was in play. The primary concern was valid and the need for a great spectacle in the USA to spread the game Stateside can't have been far from his mind.

The football fraternity often finds change hard to accept. One manager who had utilised the back-pass rule in a positive way was Arrigo Sacchi. Defenders in his Milan side used the goalkeeper to shift the point of attack with a quick pass back and throw out. He was in favour of the new rule and understood FIFA's need to 'make the game more vivacious'. Like most others, he suggested that an attitude change was just as important as rule changes. If coaches and players did not feel the need to reduce time-wasting, they would find other ways than passing back to the keeper.

Another way that managers and coaches could combat the rule change would be to bring in a defender playing the *libero* or sweeper position. This had been used on the continent more regularly, but Bobby Robson had used a version of it during Italia 90 with some success. Players like Laurent Blanc excelled in this role and his natural ability on the ball could possibly prevent teams needing to pass back to the keeper. Or teams could just stick with 4-4-2 and kick their long balls even further down the pitch.

With the rule set in place, and clarification issued to state that players could use their head or chest to return the ball to the goalkeeper legally, the Olympics began and the players, at first, struggled to adapt. Understandably, it would take outfield players time not to rely on their goalkeeper to get them out of trouble. Between the posts, goalkeepers also had the chance to become an even more important contributor to the game.

Italy faced the United States in the first ever game that used the new Law XII. It stated that goalkeepers will be punished with an indirect free kick for handling a back pass kicked to them. Blatter and the law makers had to quickly regroup and ensure that the wording of the rule was not open to any loopholes that creative footballers could circumvent, such as lying on the pitch and heading the ball along the ground.

Reporting on the opening game of the Olympic football tournament, Ken Jones, writing for *The Independent*, said that the rule might require footballers to use their brains while playing the game. Added to this was the obvious contempt that he had for the 'philistines in English football' who were so perturbed by this rule change. He revelled in the skill of the Italian goalkeeper Francesco Antonioli, who was able to avoid the close attentions of a striker with moves that would rival some Premier League players. Until, of course, Antonioli was undone by the new rule, resulting in a goal from the indirect free kick.

In England, the creation of the Premier League did not mean that the style of football changed overnight. Direct tactics were still fashionable. Full-blooded tackles were still encouraged. Determination was still a desirable attribute. Adding the new back-pass rule into the English football domain had the potential to cause absolute chaos. That is exactly what British players and managers predicted. In the pages of *Shoot*, the likes of Gerry Creaney, Bruce Grobbelaar, Neville Southall and Peter Shreeves gave their opinions. Creaney, who was banging goals in for Celtic, was positive about the move and felt like the game would open up and become more attacking. As you can imagine, Grobbelaar and Southall were far from happy. Liverpool's number one was tired of the myriad of goalkeeping rule changes that had come before, so did not expect this one to have any benefit either. His opposite number across the city was another that thought the long ball could become even more prevalent with goalkeepers now encouraged to clear the ball.

Fan voice was certainly one of the mainstays of magazines in the early 90s. Pages of letters in *World Soccer, When Saturday Comes* and the weekly *Shoot* and *Match*, gave a flavour of the voice from the terraces – a voice that seemed to be reducing in volume in the eyes of club owners and league bosses. In response to the new back-pass rule, the fans were clearly not part of the goalkeepers' union. Respondents had little sympathy for the most protected players on the pitch. Clearly, they had little time for their complaints about the possibility of being fouled by onrushing players chasing down a back pass. Most were content with leaving goalkeepers to sort themselves out, avoid the desire to dribble in their own box and get the ball forward.

During the opening weeks of the Premier League there were a few calamities from back passes. Some resulted in goals, others just total embarrassment for all involved. It was like players had been asked to take part in a totally new game. All their skill and knowledge had been lost in the floundering around the new rules.

Simon Tracey is not a name that is synonymous with the Premier League, but his antics with the ball at his feet are too famous to exclude. Video footage of the incident in a Sheffield United v Spurs match is remarkable. Real end-of-the-season video nasties fodder. A simple pass is played back to Tracey. There is very little danger anywhere. He has time and space to hoof the ball long up the pitch, where there was certainly a tall, lumbering striker waiting to knock the ball on. However, the Sheffield United keeper decided that was not the best option. And Spurs thought it was probably a good idea to press the ball. So, they did.

With a single touch to his right Tracey beckoned danger right into his path. As the onrushing Spurs forward closed in on him, he made the inexplicable decision to try and turn back in the opposite direction. The issue was his touch, which was exactly what you would expect from a goalkeeper in 1992.

Now it was a foot race to the ball. Tracey took another touch. By now they were both outside the 18-yard box. Kick it into touch, Simon. Hoof it. Do anything.

He half dribbled through the tackle and ended up running the ball right into the hands of the ball boy. Who obviously held on to the ball for far too long. Meanwhile, another Spurs player had charged over to Tracey trying to take a quick throw. The goalkeeper had abandoned his post so surely it was an opportunity to score. Tracey realised this quite quickly and performed a well-timed wrestling move to stop the play. In the chaos, the linesman barely had a chance to flag as he was almost taken out too.

Finally, the carnage came to an end. Tracey ended up getting a red card for his wrestling efforts. Not the best way to show that the new rule was going to increase the attacking output of teams. Well, maybe with this level of chaos it was inevitable that more goals would be scored.

Tracey wasn't the only player who ended up falling foul of the new rule. Goalkeepers up and down the leagues were getting caught out by the simple instruction to not pick the ball up from a back pass. Commentators were primed and ready to stick the boot into defenders who were in two minds with the new rule. They had their scripts ready and weren't afraid to use them. John Motson did just that when he pointed the finger at Roger Joseph of Wimbledon for being 'in two minds' as Lee Chapman hunted him down in the box, robbed him of the ball and found the net. Most defenders were unsure what to do when Chapman was bearing down on them.

There were countless other examples of strikers putting defenders and goalkeepers under pressure to force mistakes. It was much more interesting to watch a defence put under pressure than the sight of a striker making a half-hearted attempt to make the keeper pick the ball up. While there was not a huge increase in the number of goals, the speed and flow of the game changed completely.

Added to the mix was the fact that we got to witness grown men throwing themselves at the ball to defend indirect free kicks. Standing on the ball, players would have to perfect the short roll or touch to an onrushing team-mate who was about to burst the net or find the depths of the car park. Such glorious sights had not existed before 1992 and surely that alone is worth the price of the rule change.

As with any sport, there always ends up being a huge focus placed on individuals. In most cases they may have gotten most of the criticism, but a lot of teams did not adjust to the faster pace of the league. Where teams had relied on resetting after a back pass, a clearance from the goalkeeper meant that everyone had to be ready to run again.

Leeds and Nottingham Forest were two teams that struggled in the first Premier League season. Forest struggled so much that it ended with their relegation to the First Division and the departure of Brian Clough. Reigning champions Leeds finished 17th in the league.

Despite the difficulties and embarrassments suffered by players, the rule was here to stay, so players and managers had to make relevant adjustments.

Ultimately, they still had to ensure they were more organised than their opponents. Adapting to the new back-pass rule was just another facet of the game. Goalkeepers were players after all.

Time passed and goalkeepers adjusted to their new role in the side with the ball at their feet. Often, they would get the ball tied up in their feet and create a bit of drama in the crowd with a last-second clearance. Usually, they were happy to clear the ball downfield for a striker to flick on or a midfielder to compete for the second ball. All these things added to the game.

The desired effect of the new rule was to reduce time wasting. Unfortunately, it did not have a measurable impact on how much time was wasted. Goals did increase in USA 94 from the low numbers of Italia 90, but this was more in line with the usual goal tally at a World Cup. As ever, there was no magic bullet.

One thing that the new rule did achieve was removing the endless back and forth between goalkeeper and defender. This was no longer a legitimate tactic to finish a game. Teams would have to be much more careful in possession in the latter stages of games, rather than letting the clock tick down with meaningless exchanges in the box. So, in terms of improving the spectacle, it could be argued that the back-pass rule was a real success.

Moving forward into the late 90s, goalkeepers were becoming much more part of a team's build-up play and those with the technical ability could act as another passer from the back line. Progressive coaches could use goalkeepers to reset an attack or allow their side to get back into shape. In effect, it became an even more important position on the pitch.

Modern-day goalkeepers have taken this almost to the extreme. Dribbling past players in their box. Executing Cruyff turns to evade the press from an attacker. All these things would have been unimaginable even in 1990 (unless you were Colombian goalie René Higuita). Now, managers are encouraging these actions. Goalkeepers like Ederson of Manchester City take risks that 30 years ago would have been taken by the team's most creative player only. Now, the man between the posts has become another creative outlet. These developments could never have been predicted back in 1992, but with tactical innovations from inventive coaches it shows that the attitude to the rules can have as big an impact as the rules themselves. And in the case of the back pass, keepers certainly can kick it.

6

Money, Money, Money:
The summer transfer explosion

FOOTBALL, LIKE any major sport, is tied to
social, cultural, and political change. The end of the
1980s saw huge political upheaval as the Cold War
ended and Germany was reunified. Across Europe
the landscape was changing. The evolution of the
European Economic Community into a fully fledged
single market for member nations was in full flow,
with a major revision of the 1957 Treaty of Rome.
The act would set out the creation of a single market
in Europe by 1992.

The Maastricht Treaty was signed in February
1992, before coming into full effect just over 18 months
later. It meant that anyone who held nationality in a
member state would be a member of the European

Union (EU). This would prove to be transformative for the lives of European citizens, meaning they were able to travel and work across a large section of the continent with freedom.

Similarly, as citizens of the union, footballers would be able to move around much more freely than before. League rules around the number of non-national players would have to be changed, allowing a much larger number of players to move between clubs.

UEFA had already started this process, albeit with a certain degree of confusion, as they sought to reclassify players and their nationalities in European competitions. The rule sought to allow teams to field up to five foreign-born players instead of four. The difference would be that two of those five players would have to have lived in the club's country of origin for five years.

World Soccer (February 1992) believed the change would create a system in which young players were highly coveted, but were then left while they waited to become 'national' players. They listed examples of players who were already under the umbrella of such practices. Jamie Forrester, who became a journeyman striker, was signed by Auxerre for four years and Ivan

De La Peña, 15 years old in 1992, was already in the Barcelona system.

The problem with this rule was UEFA's classification of players in Wales, Scotland and Ireland as being foreigners. This would obviously cause a huge problem for many teams in England and the core of British players that turned out in the First Division.

The rule did not last long, and a U-turn came months later. The confirmation now was that domestic and European Cup rules would be separate. It meant that each individual federation was able to set the number of foreign players permitted in each league. Amongst all of this, the European Commission was pushing for total deregulation in Europe to the effect that a team of 11 foreign players could be fielded by anyone in any league.

In his column for *World Soccer* at the beginning of the 1992/93 season, Keir Radnedge was not convinced by UEFA's stance. By allowing freedom of movement and divorcing their own competition rules from that of domestic leagues, they were in effect giving the EU the opportunity to implement the new freedom of movement laws set by Brussels. As you can imagine, at this time, it was a seismic change in football to have the prospect of moving from a limited number of foreign players in the matchday squad to the floodgates opening.

As the most celebrated league in European football, Serie A was well positioned to adapt its foreigner restrictions to benefit its clubs. Having watched the Dutch trio of Van Basten, Gullit and Rijkaard succeed at Milan, Brehme, Matthäus and Klinsmann star for Inter and Diego Maradona take middling Napoli to the *Scudetto*, the Italian FA knew of the benefit international stars would bring to the popularity of the game. And we all know that popularity usually generates one thing: money.

Silvio Berlusconi – the influential media tycoon and owner of AC Milan – was no stranger to vast sums of money, and he was more than happy to spend it on players for his managers. The triumvirate of Dutch stars were still performing even after the appointment of Fabio Capello and the superb 1991/92 unbeaten season. Obviously, this wasn't enough for Berlusconi, and he wanted to complete a league and European Cup double. To do so he was about to fund the most extravagant transfer spending seen in football.

For Silvio had a vision. His manager did not necessarily share this vision. Berlusconi concluded that to succeed at home and abroad he would need a Milan A and Milan B. Both as good as one another and with the ability to dominate. The media magnate wanted 40 players on the books. Capello, about to test his team in Europe for the first time after the previous season's ban, wanted 22. There would only be one winner. Sacchi would certainly not have been impressed by Berlusconi's meddling.

Brian Glanville, writing in *World Soccer*, highlighted Milan's spending and suggested what was to come. Glanville wrote that footballers would be concentrated 'in a handful of clubs, where they might not even have a regular game'. Prophetic to say the least, providing an insight into the talent filtering up, not down, with the freedom of movement and seemingly endless supplies of cash.

In a league rich with exceptional footballers, Serie A also had other wealthy owners, none more so than the Agnelli family. The ruling class of Italian football as custodians of Juventus, the Agnellis bankrolled many top signings as their club dominated the domestic game, and famously became the first club to have won all the UEFA affiliated competitions. They wanted to challenge at the top of the table, and they were not about to let Milan swallow up all Europe's elite talent.

At this time, the Premier League had just about come into existence and La Liga was certainly not spending money in the way the Italians had over the previous three or four years. It was clear football was changing as owners such as Bernard Tapie, Berlusconi's equal in France, and even the TV station Canal+ who had bought Paris Saint-Germain, were willing to go to exceptional financial lengths to compete on the biggest stage. A frenzy was about to begin.

Despite their promises, and deals possibly agreed during the season, it was neither Milan, Marseille nor Juventus who got the summer spending started. Instead, it was Inter Milan who were still transitioning from the end of the highly successful Giovanni Trapattoni era. They had also allowed their three German stars to leave.

Andreas Brehme remembers the time well. He told this author that, 'every party must end, and when Trapattoni left in the summer to Juventus, I had a signed contract with Barcelona, but Barca couldn't free up the third place for a foreign player, so I ended up with Real Zaragoza, which at that time was also a huge club.' Balancing foreign players in the squad was an added layer to the manager's role and one that could prove to be difficult with players that had been successful.

Alongside Brehme, Lothar Matthäus had won the *Scudetto* under Trapattoni in 1989, as well as the UEFA Cup in 1991 after being joined by compatriot Jurgen Klinsmann. The problem for Inter's German stars was that the team had finished eighth and been knocked out at the first hurdle in their defence of the UEFA Cup.

Inter wanted to refresh their squad with a new manager arriving so the club did not wait long to bring in their first signing: Igor Shalimov for £8m from Foggia. He had starred for Zdenêk Zeman and his crazy attacking system that saw his side outscored only by Milan but have the second-worst defence in the league. The transfer became the second-most expensive in world football, behind only Roberto Baggio's record-breaking deal from Fiorentina to Juventus.

Karl-Heinz Rummenigge (ex-Inter and then Bayern vice-president) was not convinced and stated that the three new signings for Inter were 'not as good quality as Matthäus and Brehme' and that in Italy it is the foreign players that pay when it comes to transfers. They are the ones that must leave if things don't go well. At that point, owners were as concerned with flashing their cash as with filling the squad with quality players.

Having the most expensive player in the world in your squad is like a badge of honour. It made the team more marketable and made sure that fans were in no doubt about the club's ambition. It was not lost on Berlusconi that it was rivals Juventus who held that status. So, Berlusconi set about correcting that with an almost season-long pursuit of Jean-Pierre Papin, Marseille and France's star forward and one of Europe's elite. He had just won the *Ballon d'Or* after all.

If this was a marker, a real statement of intent, Milan and Berlusconi had done nothing to hide the deal from the watching football public. In fact, earlier in the season, Marseille chairman Bernard Tapie commented on speculation saying that if Capello wanted his star striker they would have to part with their three Dutch stars as payment!

After months of not-so-secret speculation, thanks to Tapie's ambition to knock down what he had built, and build it again, a deal was all but agreed in February 1992, and Papin left Marseille. A terrific servant to the club, but now he would be playing in the best league in the world with a hefty, world-record £10m price tag. Papin commented on the transfer at the time, saying that he was joining 'the greatest club in the world'. He was not far wrong.

Milan were getting a player at the peak of his powers. Papin was a superb striker. Bursting with skilful movement, pace and aggression around the penalty box, and with a tendency for a ferocious volley, he could be a superb foil for the talismanic Van Basten, or indeed, his heir. Whatever his role may be, this was a huge statement from a club that had just gone a full season unbeaten.

Another man the *Rossoneri* had been chasing throughout the season was Dejan Savićević from Red Star Belgrade, who were proving to be a feeder club for the league. Highly coveted across Europe, Savićević's deal was done before the end of the season and he arrived at the San Siro in the summer. Part of the incredible Red Star Belgrade side that beat Marseille on penalties in the 1991 European Cup

Final, he was a supremely gifted attacking midfielder and was thought of as an heir to Ruud Gullit in the side.

Concluding these deals during the previous season allowed Milan to steal a march on their rivals and it would be Juventus who were about to step into the market to strengthen a side that had finished six points behind Milan. If they were going to rediscover their glories of the 70s and 80s they needed to keep pace and they did.

So, it would be Juventus's turn to break the world transfer record. The man to lead the line with Baggio was Gianluca Vialli. The fee was even bigger than Papin's, at £12m. After Sampdoria had reached the final of the European Cup and lost, it was clear that Vialli was about to sign for one of the league's biggest (and richest) clubs. Vialli had a great goalscoring record at Samp and his partnership with Roberto Mancini gave a glimpse into what could be possible alongside Baggio.

Since the two richest clubs in Italy were battling it out for signings, it made total sense that they would eventually be fighting for the same player. Having secured their first choice striking targets, they both turned their attention to a young star: Gianluigi Lentini.

While there was reckless abandon in Italy, other nations' spending was much more measured in comparison. France, Spain, Germany and the newly minted teams of the Premier League were effectively buying players at the level of Milan's substitutes. There were of course big-name signings in those leagues, but the finances involved were not at the same level.

Marseille were the most dominant team in France having won four Ligue One titles in a row. Bernard Tapie, their own Berlusconi, was intent on making his side as strong as possible to challenge on all fronts. He was, like his Italian rival, obsessed with claiming European glory and would stop at nothing to do so.

In the transfer market, Tapie's resources were bolstered by the record sale of Papin. Initially, the deal hinged on Zvonimir Boban, who impressed on loan at Bari in 1991/92, moving in the opposite direction. The deal was beneficial for both parties, Marseille got a highly prized young player in Boban, and it meant one less foreign player for Capello to have to squeeze on to the pitch. However, Boban had other ideas and wanted to stay in Italy and fight for his place at Milan. Although, with a team full of quality players and six other contracted foreign players, a path to the first team was not easy.

Before the arrival of any new players there were departures from the Stade Velodrome. Chris Waddle, a player worshipped by the home fans, was allowed to leave for Sheffield Wednesday in a £1m deal. Trevor Steven was also allowed to return to Rangers after a single season on the south coast. Marseille made a loss of over £3m in a year on Steven and showed the sheer abandon with which owners were willing to spend, and lose, on players in the coming years.

So, with the decks clear, Marseille cashed the Papin cheque and made the move to strengthen their attack. They looked to Italy first and signed veteran striker Rudi Völler from Roma. Like Milan, the team from the capital had an excess of foreign stars. Defender Aldair and Thomas Hassler were joined by Sinisa Mihajlovic, part of the Red Star Belgrade exodus and Atalanta's Argentinian striker, and man with perfect flowing locks, Claudio Caniggia. Völler, in no mood to be competing for a starting role every week, fled and sought to establish himself again after, by his standards, an underwhelming goalscoring season.

To partner Völler, Marseille completed the signing of Alen Bokšić from Ligue One side Cannes. Having burst on to the scene with Hajduk Split and being selected for Italia 90 at age 20, Bokšić played a single game in 1991/92. Undeterred, Marseille pressed on with the signing and added him to the ranks. The new-look strike force had support at the back with the additions of a 21-year-old Fabien Barthez from Toulouse and defender Marcel Desailly from Nantes.

Tapie was not shy when it came to spending money and he certainly lived up to his reputation here. The problem for Tapie, and Marseille, was that his desperation for success at all costs meant the club paid the ultimate price at the end of the season, as after a match-fixing scandal they were stripped of their ill-gotten league title, banned from European competition and eventually, after a protracted case with the authorities, relegated.

These huge investments in superstars have become commonplace for the biggest clubs in world football. The constant barrage of transfer rumours that swirl around social media and bombard us on television are a hook to draw fans in. A promise that the club means something to the owner because of the amount they spend. Investment like this has become the norm in modern football, but you can see the roots of it here, as the prizes for success grew. Rich owners had to protect their assets and try to guarantee the biggest variable in football: success.

Further north, in Paris, for so long indifferent to their football team, another spending spree was about to begin. Canal Plus – a television empire that shows that growth in this sector in the late 1980s and 90s was akin to the tech boom of the late 90s and the streaming boom of the late 2010s – had invested heavily in Paris Saint-Germain, which meant that there was another season of significant reinforcements in the capital.

After a respectable third-place finish in 1991/92, and rising attendances, PSG strengthened their defence with the signing of goalkeeper Bernard Lama and defenders Jean-Luc Sassus and Alain Roche, but it would be two forwards who caught the eye. The departure of Christian Perez to Monaco meant PSG had sold their top scorer from the previous season. Now with funds from his sale, PSG raided the same team for a player that, along with the likes of Ronaldo and later Thierry Henry, would define the role of a number nine: George Weah.

Born in Liberia and signed by Arsene Wenger for Monaco in 1988 for £12,000, after a recommendation from Cameroon boss Claude Le Roy, Weah was one of the most coveted strikers in the world. During his time at Monaco, he had been named African Footballer of the Year, won domestic cups and made an appearance in the Cup Winners' Cup of 1992. It seemed a surprise that Monaco would allow him to leave for a close rival, but they had to fund the signing of a replacement, another striker who had come to define the forward position; Jurgen Klinsmann.

Both strikers had immense talent but filled different roles on the pitch. Klinsmann was a striker that played as a target man, link man or a poacher in the box. Weah was blessed with immense dribbling ability and strength all over the pitch. The way that he picked the ball up from deep and drove towards defences was a valuable skill. He was not a player that would be hanging around in the centre of the pitch waiting for delivery from the wingers. This ability would help to shape the way that modern tactics evolved, using a striker who could be involved in all stages of play and could also have the strength to play up front alone.

At £5m, Weah was the seventh-most expensive signing that summer and the most expensive player to move to a team outside Italy. Klinsmann cost half that, but did command a £500,000 a year salary, which in 1992 was a substantial amount of money in the football world. The German was not without his suitors and had been tracked for most of the summer by PSG and Real Madrid, who were desperate to end the empire that Johan Cruyff had built at the Nou Camp. At this point, the domination of Spanish league football continued to be centred around Real Madrid and Barcelona. In 1992, it was Barcelona's turn to dominate after the great Real Madrid side of the mid to late 80s had won five titles in a row. Unlike more recent history, Barcelona and Real Madrid were not the transfer behemoths they are today. Obviously, there were star names with big price tags attached in the 1980s, such as Bernd Schuster, Gary Lineker and Hugo Sanchez, but the only record breaker was the signing of Diego Maradona to Barcelona in 1982. That obviously didn't last long and Maradona left for Napoli in 1985.

The summer of 1992 was one of relative inactivity by the two Spanish giants with both teams' spending totalling less than the price of David Platt. It didn't matter too much to Barcelona, who were still reaping the benefits of the transfers in the summer of 1988, Cruyff's first season in charge. Each season after that, Cruyff had signed one major player to add to the nucleus of his side: Koeman in 1989, Stoichkov in 1990 and Richard Witschge in 1991. He didn't feel the need to do that this time after lifting the club's first European Cup in 1992.

Real Madrid's task was the same one, of replacing the outgoing striker, Hugo Sanchez. The new arrival was another South American; Ivan Zamorano. A £3m signing from Sevilla, the Chilean had had a good season there and earned his move to join a side that was looking to knock Barca off their perch. In truth, Zamorano was a replacement for Sanchez in position only, as it would be very difficult to replace one of the greatest footballers of all time.

The desire of both clubs to challenge Italian domination was not fulfilled until later in the 1990s and early 2000s with the Galactico era at Real Madrid and equally extravagant expenditure at Barcelona.

Both of those more modern periods have similarities with the behaviour of the top clubs in the summer of 1992. Why be content with what you have when you can continually add more and more to the playing squad?

German clubs benefitted from the vast array of players being signed by Italian clubs. With the restrictions on foreign players relaxed, but still in force, German players plying their trade in Italy found themselves on the fringes at their clubs. Having once been the players that Italian clubs wanted to fill their teams with, now it was time for them to move on. As mentioned, Marseille and Monaco benefited with the signings of Völler and Klinsmann respectively, but the domestic clubs were able to bring home players at very modest fees as Italian clubs reduced their numbers.

So, with other clubs concerned with the middle of the market that summer, Milan and Juventus continued to chase Lentini. His superb performances in Torino's journey to the UEFA Cup Final (ultimately ending in defeat to Ajax) led to both clubs wanting to sign the youngster. In teams that were now full of continental stars, it seemed strange that a homegrown player would be so sought-after. But, as with big clubs these days, the best players filter up.

After the expected and protracted bidding war, Milan announced the signing of Gianluigi Lentini from Torino for £13m. The move caused much consternation in Turin, with Torino fans protesting in the streets. The reaction if he had signed for city rivals Juventus would surely have been much worse. Really, Juventus were only at the bidding table to drive up the price for a player who was yet to really show his full potential. They were testing Milan's mettle. Berlusconi, as ever, was bullish and undeterred, ensuring that he would not be beaten by his team's closest rivals.

Lentini was nowhere near the standard of Vialli or Papin; he was unproven at the very highest level, yet to become a regular for the national team and weaker than the other creative players amongst Milan's ranks. It was a transfer that just stated Milan's financial power, especially after a title in an unbeaten season.

Undeterred by this episode, Juventus spent freely. Another star of Italia 90 joined Trapattoni's new-look side as David Platt arrived from relegated Bari for £6.5m. That Bari side had spent close to £12m on players in the 1991/92 season and somehow managed to end up relegated. Juventus were happy to pick up the pieces and acquired a player that had proved himself in Italy despite his club's circumstances.

As the third *stranieri* (foreign-born player), it looked like Platt would play a prominent role in midfield – until the waters were muddied by the arrival of German attacking midfielder Andreas Moller from Frankfurt. When the talented German signed for a fraction of Platt's fee at £2.6m, Juventus now had four foreign players in the squad. It meant Trapattoni had a selection dilemma every week. Add to that the fact his two foreign central defenders, Jurgen Kohler and Julio Cesar, had formed a formidable partnership in strengthening the defence; it was clear that someone would have to miss out.

Interestingly, the fee Juventus paid for Platt was significantly higher than the one paid by Lazio for Paul Gascoigne. Originally, Gazza should have signed for Lazio for a sum in the region of £8.5m which, if it had gone through in the summer of 1991, would have made Gascoigne the second most expensive plater in the world after Roberto Baggio. Instead, he arrived in Lazio for £1m less than his England team-mate. Gazza features heavily later.

Juventus continued to bolster their squad with the arrival of two young Italians: Dino Baggio from Torino and Fabrizio Ravanelli from Reggiana. The lesser-known Baggio would emerge as one of the stars of the season and Ravanelli displayed glimpses of the goalscoring he would be known for in years to come.

While these European giants were fighting it out at the top of the table, English teams were way down the food chain. Just returning to Europe after the club ban in the aftermath of Heysel, English clubs' finances were nowhere near that of their European neighbours. It would take a long time for the Premier League to catch up with the clubs that were signing players at the very top of the market, but once the television money started rolling in, wages and transfer fees sky-rocketed.

Across Europe, the perfect storm was taking place and the summer of 1992 is indicative of these sweeping changes. The year was a real changing of the guard around Europe in terms of player regulations and the amount of money that was about to flood the game. It was clear that one country was clearly out in front when it came to attracting the best talent.

In Italy, if Juventus and Milan wanted a player then other teams need not apply. It made them the two most dominant teams in a fiercely competitive field. The parity which had grown in the 1980s, and had seen teams such as Roma, Hellas Verona and Napoli win the domestic title, was being eroded. The spending power of the Agnellis and Berlusconi was far greater than that of the other clubs. It did not deter other clubs from spending wilfully, but it would take time for them to become competitive.

Between 1992 and 1999, Milan and Juventus shared eight league titles: Milan winning five to Juve's three. The money spent during the early years of the decade set up the teams for victory. Their success was not restricted to domestic competitions, as Milan featured in three consecutive Champions League finals, followed by Juventus in the next three. The biggest league in the world had a team in the final for six consecutive seasons, and if you look back to the 1980s, it was eight out of the last ten. Clearly, money talks.

7

The Birth of the Starball: Here comes the Champions League

THE CHAMPIONS League is part of the fabric of the modern game. A competition synonymous with the best players, managers and teams. The roll call of winners since 1992 is a who's who of the greatest club sides of a generation. Modern players such as Messi and Ronaldo have come to define their careers with incredible performances in this league, while managers like Jose Mourinho, Pep Guardiola and Jurgen Klopp have given their clubs memorable nights and lifted trophies.

Winning the Champions League has become a yardstick for big club success. Look at Manchester City under the reign of Guardiola, and even the managers that came before him. Despite five Premier

League titles in a little over a decade, the Champions League still eludes them. To the west, Liverpool have won only one Premier League title since its inception. In the same period, they have been victorious in two Champions League finals, while being on the wrong side on another three occasions. Still, they can hold those two European victories higher than any other Premier League title because it is *the* trophy to win.

Before the introduction of a league stage in 1991/92, the European Cup was a straight knockout. As you can imagine this brought about some very interesting draws in the early stages of a competition that was all about the domestic champions battling it out. For the fans, those early rounds could be fraught with danger. Neutrals on the other hand had the chance to watch a big name fall to relative minnows. As you can imagine, clubs and owners grew tired of this format. Not always for sporting reasons either.

A European Cup was the brainchild of Gabriel Hanot and Jacques Ferran of French newspaper *L'Equipe*. Both men had found common ground with the idea of teams from around Europe playing each other to determine which team was the best on the continent. Post-war, it was vital that a unified Europe showed strength and what better way than to explore this through sport? Hanot pondered on who was the best team in Europe in *L'Equipe* and had a burning desire to find out. He envisaged a European league format that would see teams leave their domestic league for a season to compete against the best in Europe. Ferran was inspired by the South American Championship of Champions. This was a club competition that sought to crown the best on the continent. Ferran and Hanot knew Europe needed an equivalent.

Despite these dreams, and ratification from UEFA in March 1955, it was not all plain sailing. In his book *The Undisputed Champions of Europe*, Steven Scragg outlines the resistance from British authorities who 'refused to be party to these new and unsettling innovations'. It all sounds very similar to fan reaction to a lot of innovations in football; the Premier League, the back-pass rule, the Champions League. Change in football is often hard to stomach, but it is always inevitable.

And that change did come, starting in the 1955/56 season. Although initially there were no English teams in the tournament, Hibs were the first British team to appear. Real Madrid were the first winners of a competition that they would come to dominate, starting off with five consecutive titles. That team, another collection of Galacticos in white, featured the likes of Ferenc Puskas, Alfredo Di Stefano and Francisco Gento.

Manchester United would be the first team from England to take part in the competition, duly losing to the might of Madrid in the semi-final in 1957. Tragedy struck United the following season in the Munich air disaster with 23 crew, players, staff and journalists losing their lives. A club was robbed of a generation of incredible talent and families and friends lost their loved ones.

Over time, the competition grew, with football associations from around the continent signing up to pit their domestic champions against the best Europe had to offer. The prize was not spread around as much season-by-season as would be the case later. Fewer transfers allowed teams to stay together for longer, thus preserving a side at their peak. That meant these teams were dominant domestically too: remember, this was still a cup for champions.

Between the tournament's inception in 1955 and 1980, there were 25 finals held. Those finals were won by just 11 different clubs, seven of which won titles back-to-back. It was an incredible period for football with club sides from seven countries emerging victorious. This competition truly was the pinnacle of football for league champions. Now, as we know, it is no longer preserved for the champions, and for some clubs is seen as a financial necessity rather than the chance to compete against the elite.

English sides dominated the competition in the late 1970s and early 1980s. To have three different teams winning six consecutive finals was incredible. No other nation had dominated the tournament in the same way. If you include Liverpool's 1984 win, then English sides won seven out of eight finals in that period. Liverpool also played in the 1985 final against Juventus, meaning that English teams had appeared in eight of a possible nine finals between 1977 and 1985. After the events at Heysel in 1985, English teams were not allowed to compete in European competition for five years and Liverpool were banned for six.

English teams were on top of the pile at that point, so over the next few years teams without the same reputation lifted the trophy. Broadcasters quickly lost interest in the competition and failed to show any of the European Cup Finals live until English clubs returned. In the interim, things changed thanks to a change in ownership of an Italian great.

Silvio Berlusconi was no ordinary football owner. He certainly would have looked out of place picking up sandwiches from a buffet in the directors' box of any English club in the 1980s. Berlusconi was different. He had ambition and opinions. Lots of opinions and most of them involved his side having more opportunities to win while getting rich at the same time.

The concept of a European Super League was not new. Like Hanot's original vision, the plan for a league format on the continent had also been raised in the 1970s. UEFA, now a powerful organisation, ensured the challenge was defeated and the status quo was maintained.

Football, as with many areas in the 1980s, was beginning to become more lucrative for owners. Television rights were crucial in securing the financial stability of clubs. Berlusconi knew that if his side were not in Europe's premier competition then their earning power decreased. He set about righting perceived injustices by approaching other European clubs and taking his proposals to UEFA. Of course, Berlusconi's policies were Milan-centric and aimed to ensure that his club would benefit from guaranteed games and earnings. The plan was to create a European league that would take teams out of their domestic leagues and place them into his new competition. UEFA saw this off once more and even Berlusconi realised that this was possibly not the best way to get clubs and the authorities on board.

Change can be difficult and messy. It is often instigated at the behest of the self-serving few and usually means someone, somewhere is about to get rich. That was certainly the case with Berlusconi, who had made his money in property and was the owner of a television company that always needed programming. A European Super League certainly fitted the bill. Now, an organisation could not bend to the whim of one man, but change was afoot. While English clubs were fighting over their own possible super league, the wheels had started to turn in the European corridors of power.

Having enlisted Saatchi and Saatchi to stake his claim for a new European Super League, Berlusconi pressed on with his plan. Alex Flynn was the executive put in charge of creating a blueprint for a new European Super League. Flynn knew that more matches between the best teams was what the big television markets wanted and needed. His plan was to create an 18-team league with two or three clubs from the major nations, plus teams from other, smaller nations. The plan was rebuffed. Flynn went on to co-author *The Secret Life of Football*, a book that showed how football, especially in England, was bereft of ideas and vision. Clearly, the desire for change was increasing and it was just a matter of in which form it would be accepted.

While Berlusconi was jostling for power with UEFA, there was a plan being drawn up in Scotland by the general secretary of Rangers. His name was Campbell Ogilvie and he was about to change European football forever.

Rangers had been the dominant side domestically at the back end of the 1980s but were not progressing in Europe. As with Milan and Berlusconi, ideas often come out of perceived adverse conditions. So, at a board meeting, Ogilvie and fellow directors discussed how Rangers could preserve their place in European competition for longer. A plan was drawn up and

Vinnie Jones decides to nail a Wimbledon shirt to one of Sky Sports' Premier League posters.

One last look as Gary Lineker leaves the pitch against Sweden in his final match for England.

England line up before the disappointing 2-1 defeat to Sweden at Euro '92.

The jubilant Danes mob Kim Vilfort after scoring his second goal in the final.

Milan's world record signing Gianluigi Lentini holds off Marseille's Jocelyn Angloma in the 1993 UEFA Champions League Final.

George Weah joins his new team-mates David Ginola and Bernard Lama after his £5m move from Monaco.

Mark Hateley and Marcel Desailly chase the ball down in the Champions League game between Rangers and Marseille.

A. PREMIER
SHARP
SHARP
SHARP
MORSON
INTERNATIONAL
reusch
SHARP

Manchester United's domestic dominance begins with triumph in the inaugural Premier League season.

Gazza takes in the sights of Rome a year before his move to Italy.

Manchester United's class of 1992 celebrate victory in the FA Youth Cup Final.

shoehorned into a UEFA board meeting. Ogilvie had support from Roger Vanden Stock of Anderlecht and despite initially being rejected by UEFA, the plan was passed for the start of the 1991/92 season. The format was not what the major players intended. It started with a straight knockout stage, then a league/group stage would be introduced for the final eight teams. The top team in each group of four would then play against each other in the final, for the European Cup.

Clearly this was not what Berlusconi or his allies (Bernard Tapie of Marseille and Ramon Mendoza of Real Madrid) intended, as they could still be knocked out before this point. They wanted the format to be reversed so that there was a guaranteed number of group games before the knockout rounds commenced at the quarter-final stage. Eventually this format would be adopted, but for now this was a huge step towards the well-established Champions League we know today.

Having such a powerful and successful figure like Berlusconi pushing the agenda meant that the focus was no longer on creating a premier competition for European teams. Focus turned to ensuring the top teams played the maximum number of games, giving them a greater financial share. Simple really. All these machinations were a far cry from Ferran and Hanot's idea of finding out which team was the best on the continent.

The 1991/92 European Cup started with the usual knockout competition for the first two rounds; 32 teams from across the continent competing for the biggest prize in football. Across the first-round ties there were no shocks. Rangers were pushed close by Sparta Prague, needing away goals to triumph, but there was no jeopardy for anyone else.

Ironically, one team absent from any of the European competitions that season was Berlusconi's Milan. They had refused to complete a game against Marseille in the previous season due to floodlight failure, and so were banned.

The second round saw holders Red Star Belgrade and past winners Benfica advance, while other big names who were yet to lift the trophy joined them. Barcelona and Sampdoria were two of the stronger teams among the eight who remained, and they were placed in separate groups for the new phase of the competition.

Now the make-up of the two four-team groups was decided, every team would play the other three in their group home and away, with the group winners going into the final. Games were played across six game weeks, roughly every fortnight, but with a huge three-month break between matches two and three. This break would continue into the modern competition even after the format changed.

After a competitive group stage, apart from Panathinaikos, Barcelona and Sampdoria reached the final to be held at Wembley. For Cruyff's dream team it would be the chance to finally lift the trophy that had eluded them and prove that his methods and managerial style could triumph on the European stage. It was especially important after they had lost to Manchester United in the Cup Winners' Cup Final the year before. English teams were supposed to be weaker than their continental neighbours, but Barcelona had found that wasn't the case.

Despite their misstep in the hunt for a European trophy, Barcelona emerged victorious in the European Cup Final. It made them the last team to lift the trophy under its original name. While the tournament had been going on, UEFA tasked TEAM Marketing AG to produce a television and marketing package that they would control. From this partnership came the classic Champions League branding that we know today; the iconic anthem, instantly recognisable colour scheme and the famous 'Starball' logo. The fact that these facets remain is truly incredible and shows the power of a great brand.

This key development in the march towards the success of that first Champions League season came not from a footballing innovation, but from the allocation of television rights. As UEFA had taken over the rights to televising and advertising it meant a huge windfall for clubs. A total of around 55 per cent of the revenue would be shared between the clubs in the tournament, providing the final eight teams with a guaranteed £2.8m each. The future was here and not only was it televised, but it would also make some clubs very wealthy.

Some owners were quite content to publicly back the idea of a European Super League. One was Berlusconi and another was David Murray, chairman of Britain's biggest club at the time, Glasgow Rangers. Speaking to *World Soccer* in early 1992, Murray was adamant that Rangers would be part of any European Super League structure. He knew that the creation of the European Single Market was a game-changing proposition for clubs. Murray was, at the time, a modern chairman, a very wealthy one, and with a background of business success and acumen. The merits of these claims certainly came into question with his later decisions.

At this point though, Murray was firmly behind making Rangers a money-making operation. He knew that being part of any development in Europe was vital to keep the club relevant. The fact that his spending power was creating a chasm within Scottish football was exactly what would happen across the European game. Like most of the other rich individual football owners of the early 1990s, Murray wanted quick wins and quick fixes and was not about to sit back and be dictated to by the authorities.

When Berlusconi spoke to Keir Radnedge from *World Soccer* in May 1992, he was also bullish about his own club and their role in the European game. In his own words he stated that 'it's economic nonsense that a club such as Milan might be eliminated in the first round'. Clearly, from a footballing sense, if his club were knocked out then that was that. Not for Silvio though. He wanted more. His desire extended to the expansion of the Milan squad with the possibility of running almost a parallel team for league and cup competitions.

Taking things a step further, and a leaf out of Alan Sugar and BSkyB's book, Berlusconi's Fininvest won the television rights to show the new Champions League in Italy. The company beat the state-owned RAI and would have exclusive rights from the 1992/93 season. It seems incredible that a football club owner could push for reform of a competition and then win the television rights to it. Welcome to football economics.

Now all the formalities were out of the way, the new competition could be launched and European club football would be changed forever. It sounded easy enough.

There was a new Premier League in England, huge investment in players across Europe, changes to the back-pass law and a new competition for European football, the Champions League. Although not the first part of the tournament. That was still the European Cup. After all the jostling and proposals, UEFA ended up with a hybrid format of knockout games, which led into a Champions League phase, leading to a place in the

European Cup Final. Strangely, it would take until the 1994/95 season before the whole tournament would be known as the Champions League. Despite this, the Champions League branding was inescapable and you'd be forgiven for thinking the new format was called the UEFA Champions League from 1992/93.

Thanks to the ballooning number of member states in UEFA, the first round of the European Cup/Champions League would feature 32 teams in total. These places were taken by domestic champions. For England, the last ever First Division champions, Leeds, would take their place in the competition. They would have a somewhat controversial passage through the first round against reigning German champions Stuttgart.

Amongst all the structural changes to league and European competitions, there were also legal challenges to a wide range of legislation that UEFA used to manage its clubs. One of the main points of contention in the early 90s was the use of foreign-born players. At first, UEFA declared that anyone born outside of the club's nation of origin was classed as foreign-born. English clubs were both confused and angered by this decision. For them, it meant non-English, but British players would be classed as foreign. Most clubs had players from the home nations, often outnumbering their English counterparts. Clubs would have had their best XI severely weakened by this rule, but as you can imagine in the transitional nature of the time, changes to the rule were made. So, eventually, UEFA settled on a system. Clubs would be able to field five foreign players, but at least two must have lived in the club's country of origin for at least five years.

What happened next? Well, someone forgot about the rule and caused their team to get knocked out. Remember this was the early 90s, when change was moving so fast that even managers were having their decisions affected by ever-changing rules. Christoph Daum, manager of Stuttgart, inadvertently broke the foreign-player rule with the introduction of Jovica Simanic. For the last eight minutes of the game, Stuttgart had fielded an illegal team. They should have progressed on away goals after a 3-0 home win was followed up by a 4-1 defeat at Elland Road. Leeds protested to UEFA, who, rightly, enforced the rules and decided that the tie should be replayed. In their wisdom they decreed that the game should now be a single knockout game at a neutral venue. So, at the Camp Nou, Leeds and Stuttgart replayed the tie, but this time Leeds prevailed. A 2-1 victory meant passage into the next round and a 'Battle of Britain' match against Rangers.

Rangers passed the test against Leeds with 2-1 victories in both legs. The Scottish champions were a dominant force domestically, but Leeds' defence of their title was far from a success. Dismal performances as well as a stretched squad meant that they were out of the title race before it even began. North of the border, Rangers' spending power surpassed all their rivals and the management of Walter Smith, coupled with a potent strike force, meant they were easily the best club side in Britain at the time. They proved it with their passage into the first ever Champions League.

Rivals in their group were beaten finalists from 1991, Marseille. The reigning French champions continued to dominate at home and were ready for an assault on the European Cup to fulfil Tapie's ambitions. Jean-Pierre Papin had been the star in Marseille but was now part of the Milan super squad. Tapie, who was as passionate, rich and dominating as Berlusconi, would not allow his side to fail again. Unfazed by the loss of one of the top three strikers in Europe, he reinvested by signing goalkeeper Fabien Barthez, defensive colossus Marcel Desailly and strikers Alen Bokšić and Rudi Völler. They all proved to be inspired signings with Bokšić and Völler scoring a bagful of goals.

Dominating the French first division was one thing, but European glory was difficult to come by. They would emerge from their group with three wins and three draws, narrowly edging out Rangers by a single point. While this campaign proved to be the high point for Rangers in the Champions League, it sent Marseille to a second final in two years.

Dogged by controversy as ever, Tapie had gone too far this time and his club were accused of bribing Valenciennes players to allow Marseille to secure the league title with minimal effort and so have more time to get ready for the final in Munich. Incredibly, nothing changed for them in the lead-up to the match and they were ready to take on the victors from Group Two.

Milan had won back-to-back European Cups under Arrigo Sacchi, the man who changed Italian football. An aggressive high line and intensive pressing separated the side from others of the era. The fact they had Van Basten, Gullit and Rijkaard in attack certainly helped. Defensively they had a few greats scattered across the back line too.

After splashing a record-breaking amount of money in one summer, Milan were obviously favourites at home and abroad to lift the trophy again. Fabio Capello was in the dugout this time. He was seen as more of a company man, but he was certainly forging his own way in the game. Milan performed incredibly well under his leadership, and they proceeded to do the same in the knockout rounds of the competition, where 7-0 and 5-0 aggregate victories meant their passage to the Champions League was very straightforward. However, from there, drawn in a group of death with IFK Gothenburg, Porto and PSV Eindhoven, Milan had a decidedly more difficult path to the final than their French rivals.

One player had come to dominate the headlines for Milan in the footballing world: Marco Van Basten. Scorer of incredible goals, tap-ins and from anywhere around the box, he was the complete forward. The ultimate number nine. He was in the prime of his career as he came into the 92/93 season. He was now joined by Papin to provide him with a partner, competition for the number nine shirt and cover when he needed rest.

After an injury-plagued first season at Milan, Van Basten had a consistent record of playing a high number of games and scoring plenty of goals. He had played more than 150 games in the previous four seasons, showing he was not hampered by a nagging ankle problem. What happened over the next two seasons was tragic. For a player that was in the peak years of his career to be robbed of taking it any further was a huge loss to football and for Van Basten as a player.

While he was still playing, Van Basten did what he did best and that was score goals. He played five games for Milan and scored six goals, but all of them came in just two games: the first-round victory over Olimpija Ljubljana and the first Champions League game against Gothenburg. That game against the Swedish champions was a classic Van Basten performance. For a player who was probably the best in the world in 1992, it was fitting that he would mark his Champions League debut and the opening matchday with not only a hat-trick but four goals.

The first thing to notice when you watch the footage is the lack of sponsors on shirts. At that point, UEFA did not allow teams to display them on the front of their kits. As new contracts and deals had been signed in terms of marketing, not everything was straightforward. What it did do was showcase the brilliance of a Milan home shirt. The iconic red and black stripes with the simple adidas trefoil logo is superb. Long-sleeved versions of them in the Italian winter just add that extra bit of class.

Van Basten wasn't too concerned about the shirt he wore. His goals mattered most, and he single-handedly won this game for his team. All of them were scored from in the box. One a classic Van Basten effort, the second a penalty and the fourth involved a defensive mix-up; Gothenburg players froze while Van Basten rolled the ball into the net. The third goal was a classic.

A cross floated up towards the edge of the box. Van Basten shuffled back and adjusted his footing, getting ready to strike. He didn't just strike it; he contorted his body perfectly to execute a sublime overhead kick from just inside the box. The ball skipped off the turf and flew into the bottom corner. Memorable goals like that deserve to be scored on the biggest stage and the Champions League was about to provide that.

Marseille and Milan progressed from their Champions League groups and into the European Cup Final. The confusing naming of each part of the competition did not last too much longer and looking back it just feels like a misjudged temporary solution. Both teams were at full strength for the final and it promised to be a very tight affair.

A single goal decided the game with Basile Boli's header the decisive moment. Marseille's players and their owner paraded the huge trophy around the pitch. Tapie's dream had come true, while Berlusconi's millions could not secure a third European Cup triumph. One thing that both men had managed to achieve was giving their clubs a platform on the biggest stage. Investing their seemingly endless resources into two brilliant teams, they had also influenced an historic tournament to change.

For all the flaws within the new format, it was clearly here to stay. The additional games in the Champions League phase would prove to be too lucrative for teams to ever move away from. Guarantees are few and far between in football. Success can be cyclical so while you are on top you need to make sure you stay there. One of the main ways to do that is with more money than your competitors. So, champions from around the continent were never going to refuse the chance to bolster their bank balances.

Arguably, having more of these competitive games provided a better spectacle than the often-one-sided ties played before the latter stages of a tournament. Others might argue that the magic of those early rounds at least gave the minnows the chance to defeat the super clubs. Milan and Marseille were proving that with endless spending power, the gap between the top and the bottom was only going to increase. With a chosen few being 'guaranteed' these large sums of television money, the gap was only going to widen. These dangers were often shared by journalists and people within football, but as is frequently the case, their pleas fell on deaf ears.

The advent of the Champions League certainly brought about rapid change. The 93/94 season featured another set of preliminary and opening rounds before the two-group Champions League stage came into force. Deciding that too many of the latter group matches lacked any real competitiveness, UEFA brought back the semi-finals. This meant that the group winner would face off against the second-placed side from the opposite group. Each semi would be a single game, with the group winners given home advantage.

Milan had their moment in the spotlight once more in the 1994 final with the demolition of Johan Cruyff's dream team. It was one of the greatest performances in football, and without Baresi and Costacurta through suspension, Lentini through injury and the three non-nationals Papin, Brian Laudrup and Florin Raducioiu. This was the last final to be branded as the European Cup, or European Champion Clubs' Cup as it was also known. It seemed fitting that one of the greatest club sides of all time would emerge victorious.

From 1994, it was the UEFA Champions League for good. The format had a qualifying round for the smaller nations (or those with the lowest coefficient) and then a four-team, four-group stage that stretched through autumn into winter. Then, in spring, the knockout stage would return with a quarter-final.

By this point, and through the whole narrative of change during this period, fans had not come into the equation. Television companies and lawmakers had more power than ever. These priorities were driven by the already wealthy owners of the biggest clubs in Europe. Guaranteeing income against their investments was good business sense. For UEFA, they too benefitted with a healthy annual income generated from selling television and advertising rights.

By the time Milan returned to the final for a third consecutive year in 1995, the overall viewer numbers for the Champions League had increased to 3.64 billion. Incredibly, this was up 61 per cent from the previous season, an increase of 1.4 billion. Clearly, there was an appetite for football on television and UEFA were more than happy to provide it for the fans. As for the clubs, they couldn't be happier. Well, until they decided that they had another shot at a European Super League.

8

Golazzo: *Football Italia* arrives on Channel 4

THE SCENE was set. A league of nations, full of expensive stars and a channel new to showing football coverage was about to take England by storm. No, not the Premier League and Sky Sports. Serie A and Channel 4.

A partnership that would last a decade and brought the desire for more foreign stars and big spending that would characterise the Premier League as it dominated the world of football.

Football on television is the legacy of the changes made to the game in 1992. The removal of the back pass to bring in defensive jeopardy, super teams being created with the change in transfer approach, the new Premier League and the advent of the Champions

League all made the game more attractive to spectators around the world.

It wasn't always like this. Twenty-four-hour television coverage of football simply did not exist in 1992. News was filtered through local news, the written press, printed weekly magazines and the trusty source of Teletext. Then, every two years an international tournament would bring stars from around the world into the spectators' living rooms. These stars were spellbinding. It made fans fall in love with football time and time again.

England football and their fans had not experienced European players on their shores for several years before 1992. Manchester United certainly made up for lost time with their Cup Winners' Cup victory in 1991 against Cruyff's Barcelona. But exposure to players from around the continent was a rare occurrence.

There were of course opportunities to understand the game on the continent through publications like *World Soccer* and regular television coverage of Serie A on Sky Sports (still emerging in the early 90s) and Ligue 1, which was also shown on Sky Sports. Terrestrial television channels had not yet realised the power of football in the home, instead just enjoying the huge viewing numbers for England games at major tournaments.

The tide was turning. Alongside the formation of the Premier League, television bosses realised there was a chance to increase viewing figures if they could show more football to draw in the crowd that would normally be reserved for those biennial tournaments. Channel 4 were about to change English football, by turning their attention to the best league in the world.

While Sky were concerned with blowing ITV out of the water for Premier League rights, they had allowed the rights to Serie A to expire. Preoccupied with the protracted negotiations for the new English super league, they submitted a derisory, almost careless, offer of £500k to secure another season of arguably the best league in the world. Channel 4 got wind of this and set their stall out to bring foreign football to terrestrial television.

At the time, the league had the world's best players. Clubs were bankrolled by billionaires, and they were quick to invest their money in the most expensive players. It translated into success in Europe with Milan winning back-to-back European Cups and Sampdoria reaching the last final of the old format, only to be defeated by Barcelona.

In the UEFA Cup the Italian theme continued with Serie A clubs in four consecutive finals, including consecutive all-Italian contests. Napoli, Juventus and Inter added to their trophy cabinets with victories against Stuttgart, Fiorentina and Roma respectively. Torino lost the showpiece against Ajax in 1992. To look further past 1992, there were three more finals featuring Italians with another all-Italian affair. It truly was a league that was dominant in Europe.

A list of the star players in the league at that time was a roll call of the best players in the world. Other leagues had stars, but Serie A was on a different level. These players don't even need a first name for recognition; Baresi, Maldini, Gullit, Rijkaard, Van Basten, Baggio, Vialli, Platt: and they are just the stars from Milan and Juventus. Throughout the league there were expensive imports that elevated the competition. As mentioned, this was reflected in the Italian sides' European exploits.

Aside from Sky diverting their attention to a whole new ball game, there was another footballing reason why Channel 4 wanted the rights to show Serie A: Paul Gascoigne. The most famous player in English football had agreed a transfer to Lazio on the eve of Tottenham's FA Cup Final. A £7.5m fee was set and Gazza was primed to arrive in the capital that summer. His horror tackle on Gary Charles (in which Gazza suffered a serious knee injury) ended that dream and instead a year of rehabilitation beckoned.

Lazio did not renege on the deal, instead they renegotiated a smaller fee. Still a huge £5.5m, but now he would cost less than fellow England international David Platt, who had been plying his trade at Bari. The transfer would prove to be great timing for Channel 4, who wanted to build their new Italian football programming around Gazza. Not one to shy away from the camera after his emergence at the World Cup, Gazza (or his advisors) agreed.

So Channel 4 secured the rights for somewhere between £1.2 and £1.5m a season (remember the Sky deal was £60.8m a year). They also had a huge potential audience on terrestrial television. There was no need for subscriptions or an unsightly dish on the side of your house. It was like they had struck gold and no one had realised. The stage was set for Channel

4 to show quality football for the masses. They had a plan of how they would deliver this product to the fans and it would prove to be a monumental success.

Part one of the plan was to show a live game on a Sunday afternoon at a similar time to Sky Sports' *Super Sunday.* The plan, unbelievably really, was waved through with little fanfare. Channel 4 would be in direct competition with the new Premier League but were confident that the football would speak for itself.

During this period, most of the reporting in the English media was about the Premier League. Most publications featured a short news-in-brief section on foreign football, but this was to increase exponentially in the 1992/93 season. The access that English fans had to the league meant that they needed to be informed about this new, exotic league.

The talent that could be found in Serie A was far greater than that on domestic shores. *When Saturday Comes* even ran with the price disparity on their front cover; a grinning Frank Rijkaard gave Channel 4's £1.5m deal the thumbs-up. It was, and still is, an absolute bargain deal and probably one of the best. Channel 4 certainly reaped the benefits with a bumper television audience who had been raised on *The Big*

Match but were now about to experience *Football Italia* in all its sun-drenched colour.

Despite the relatively tiny amount of television income from abroad, a key factor in the growth of modern football, the summer of spending in Italian football had been unprecedented. Talent flowed through the league and English fans who had characterised Italian football as dull were soon to be proved wrong. Unless you were an avid reader of *World Soccer* or closely followed English clubs on their return to the continent, several players in Serie A would have passed you by. The introduction of *Gazzetta Football Italia* on Saturday mornings and the live match coverage of *Football Italia* on Sunday afternoons changed all of that. Fans' appetite for the exotic was about to explode.

So, with the rights secured, Kenneth Wolstenholme and Peter Brackley signed up to deliver the match-day commentary, and James Richardson was added to present the weekly magazine show that would form part of Channel 4's sporting offering on Saturday mornings. For those old enough to remember those days, the transition from *Transworld Sport* to *The Morning Line* (skip that one) to *Gazzetta Football*

Italia was a dream. All of this was digested before all the week's team news and coverage of the domestic game on *Football Focus*.

Gazza was a key part of this new venture from Channel 4. In the two years preceding and following Italia 90, he had become a football superstar. These days players are all over social media from the club's official media content to their personal logs of their daily activities, whether it is getting their teeth whitened or sharing new products they are involved with. The football machine worked differently in 1992. Players had deals with companies to advertise on TV or in magazines, but there was no desire to build a personal brand. The truth was most footballers wanted to make a quick buck in the days of annual wages that were closer to the hourly rate of a modern player. Gazza was no different. Mel Stein, Gazza's agent, could see the earning potential of his client so made sure that Gazza mania swept the nation from the minute he stepped off the plane in Luton in 1990.

From merchandise to hit singles, Gazza pretty much did everything. His appearances on talk shows were numerous and he really was the poster boy of English football. The affable Geordie was never far from controversy either. His antics upset managers and wound up players including his own team-mates, but there was no denying his sheer magnetism. Channel 4 had noticed too.

Neil Duncanson was making a documentary about Gazza for Channel 4 and his recovery from the horrific 1991 injury, when he had the idea to ask the Italian Football Federation to broadcast Lazio's games back in England. Michael Grade was the chief executive of Channel 4 at the time, and he was sold on the idea. Duncanson noted in an interview with the *Guardian* in 2012 that Grade bought up all the billboards next to Sky Sports' adverts for the Premier League. The wording was less than subtle but told the story: 'Watch the world's Premier League live and exclusive on Channel 4'.

Duncanson and the company he worked for, Chrysalis, boomed over this period with their sports coverage that would quickly expand to Formula 1 for ITV in the mid-90s. But, in 1992, there was only one thing on the agenda. Bringing incredible football into the homes of Brits. It would be fresh, dynamic and different. The stale football formula was about to be swept away. Culturally, the country was about to sweep the 1980s aside and football was a huge part of this.

The plan was to be inventive and creative, so the first step was for Gazza to present *Gazzetta*, a Saturday morning magazine show that would review the week in Serie A. It would feature all the goals from around the league, interviews with some of the biggest names and include some Gazza-based skits. Richardson would be the straight man to Gazza's practical joker. The odd couple didn't last long, but the seeds had been sown to produce an alternative to the staid suit jackets that had featured (and still do) on English broadcasts.

Football Italia was the main event, broadcast every Sunday afternoon with one match chosen to be shown live. For the season, the commentary duties were shared between Wolstenholme and Brackley with a rotating cast of ex-Serie A expats such as Ray Wilkins, Joe Jordan and Luther Blissett. For the 1992/93 season the broadcast was hosted in a studio in London, a far cry from the following years when the majestic stadiums became a character themselves.

The first game of the *Football Italia* coverage on Channel 4 had to involve Lazio, so the 'roadshow' made its first stop at Stadio Luigi Ferraris where Gazza's club were the visitors, taking on European Cup finalists Sampdoria, the new employers of Des Walker. The only problem was that Gazza wasn't fit to make his debut. In what should have been the Des Walker v Gazza game, it was merely Walker v the spectre of Gazza that was hanging over a mid-table Lazio team. Or something like that, anyway.

The moment was nevertheless historic. A live game on terrestrial television, on a Sunday afternoon, beaming pictures of the greatest league in the world into homes across the UK. The game itself was a classic.

Like most of the Italian teams that summer, the owners had splashed the cash to try and compete with the Milan juggernaut. Added to the marquee signing of Gascoigne, Lazio had been busy in the transfer market. They started five new signings including Aron Winter, Giuseppe Favalli, Diego Fuser and Roberto Cravero. The fifth man was a 24-year-old striker who had joined from Zdenêk Zemen's attacking express train, Foggia; Giuseppe 'Beppe' Signori.

By the end of the game, Signori was the name on everyone's lips. After an unfortunate own goal from

Diego Fuser after six minutes, the diminutive striker hit back. His two goals in three minutes put the side from the capital in front. It was a sign of things to come as Signori would go on to lift the *Capocannoniere* (top league goalscorer trophy) at the end of the season. He would repeat the feat the following season and once more in 1996.

Signori came to embody what fans loved about *Football Italia.* A more unknown name with a wealth of talent on the rise in a league that was already full of world class names. It was this strength in depth that distinguished Serie A from others in Europe. The sheer spending power of the big clubs dwarfed that of those anywhere in world football. The fact that journalists were lamenting the spending in England was partly down to the fact that the prices were inflated for the quality on offer.

At the time, *World Soccer* estimated that Serie A had accumulated talent worth over £1 billion in the preceding years. In the summer of 1992 alone, big-spending Milan had splashed out over £35m to continue to add to the wealth of talent in Italy. Clearly, it was a league that was determined to stay on top and the quality of the football was incredible. Fans of football were instantly smitten. Journalists not so much: they lamented the birth of relentless live football. Television companies didn't mind.

Channel 4 knew the coverage was a success from that first weekend and the viewing numbers were enormous. Despite being up against the Premier League and the unfair assumption that Italian football was boring, that first game brought in three million viewers. The numbers massively dwarfed those on Sky who managed around 750,000–900,000. Throughout that first season, the *Football Italia* television audiences averaged around 800,000 a week, which is incredible for live football, let alone from another country.

The idea had been for much of Channel 4's coverage to revolve around Gazza, but it would not be until the fourth game of the season that he would make his first appearance. His first few games were tentative, ensuring his knee could hold up against Italian defenders and trying to get back to full fitness after well over a year out.

Every player has their moment though and Gazza got his in the *Derby della Capitale*. He was yet to find the net for Lazio, but his performances were improving. The footballing script writers certainly had their cliches at the ready for this game. Wearing the iconic 10 shirt reserved for the most influential Italian players, Gazza saved his coming out party for the 86th minute against Roma. A deep free kick was lifted into the box by Signori. Gazza was moving toward the penalty spot. As the ball got closer, he leapt high above the Roma defence and powered a header into the back of the net. Cue pandemonium, as you can imagine. Finally, Lazio fans could celebrate owning a player with the ability of Gazza.

For Gazza, he launched himself over the advertising hoardings, arms aloft. It was almost a release from the horrific injuries, failed recovery and criticism. The tears on his return to the centre circle said it all.

In retrospect, it was a false dawn, but at the time, he had arrived. For viewers in England, having a fit and firing Gazza would've been even more of a spectacle; instead they grew to love the world's best. Italian clubs certainly did their bit in ensuring the league had the top talent.

In his book *Golazzo: The Football Italia Years,* Grade recalls those heady times. He remembers editing goal packages that often missed out important match events but showcased the quality (and sometimes unpredictability) of those early rounds of the season. Looking back, he recalls how 'the passion and colour on the terraces was a marked contrast from anything I'd ever seen in football in the UK'. There was a definite style difference as well, clear to see from those opening highlights on *Gazzetta*. The technical level of football was at a far higher level than anything on offer domestically. The concern for Grade and the team was that 'some fans in the UK considered Italian football to be "boring" but ... eventually that tag was lost with all the stars on show, and the matches were generally anything but dull.' Over those first few weeks of the 1992/93 season there were some of the most incredible results ever seen.

Milan, known for their defensive prowess and unbeaten from the season before, conceded an extraordinary ten goals in the first five games. This was almost half of their total from the previous season. Incredibly, despite their leaky defence, they won all those games, scoring 20 goals in the process. Truly amazing results saw them win 5-4, 7-3 and 5-2. The death of *catenaccio* truly was televised!

By the end of the season, Milan were crowned champions despite managing only one win in their last 11 games. An incredible statistic, but they still won the league by four points (Serie A still used two points for a win at this stage). The challengers tried to close the gap but to no avail. Big-spending Juventus could only manage a fourth-place finish so it was left to Inter to provide the competition and they secured second place.

The first season of *Football Italia* was a huge success. The draw of the league was only reinforced by the signings that Italian clubs made over that period. Clubs did not always splash out record fees like in the summer of 1992, but still hoovered up the best talent in world football. Some became world class stars, while others built on the depth of Italian sides and ensured it remained the most competitive league in the world.

It would take another four years for the transfer-fee record set by Lentini to be broken. Since the arrival of Maradona in 1984, Serie A clubs had held the record for 12 years and six transfers. Barcelona would stop that run with the signing of Brazilian superstar Ronaldo in the summer of 1996. This was then bettered soon after by Kevin Keegan's Newcastle. Signing hometown boy Alan Shearer for £15m was a huge statement for the Premier League, but it would be 20 years before a Premier League club would break the world record fee again.

Italian clubs weren't about to hang around for that long, so Inter decided to break the record by signing Ronaldo from Barcelona. Massimo Moratti, the Inter owner, spent £19.5 million on the best player in the world and he soon began to repay the fee. *Football Italia* viewers got to see him for free, live on terrestrial television. At the same time, the league featured players like Alessandro Del Piero, Oliver Bierhoff, Gabriel Batistuta, Francesco Totti, Andrei Shevchenko and Filippo Inzaghi – and they were just the forwards.

Look at Lazio under the ownership of Sergio Cragnotti. After the signing of Gazza, these are some of the players bought over the next decade; Alen Bokšić, Pavel Nedved, Christian Vieri, Marcelo Salas, Sinisa Mihajlovic, Juan Sebastian Veron, Hernan Crespo and Claudio Lopez. Huge stars brought ever increasing transfer fees at a time when English clubs were still working within more 'normal' limits. After this period in Italy, it would be Real Madrid and the Galacticos that would concern themselves with smashing transfer records every summer. Those years in Serie A might never be repeated.

The sheer number of top-quality players in the league was unsurpassed in that period and Channel 4 viewers got to see it all. The Premier League was certainly on the up, but it was now the foreign talent the league was attracting that was generating the interest. As a product it was becoming more international and that was the selling point that had made Serie A so successful. The 'League of Nations' was what people wanted to see. As a package the football on display was incredible and some of the names mentioned are legends of the game.

Over that period football was not always the main attraction of *Football Italia*. No, it was often one man: James Richardson. A man who would come to define a whole era of football for a certain group of fans, one which, despite this period being over 30 years ago, still holds a place at the pinnacle of football. His role as presenter of *Gazzetta Football Italia* evolved with the viewer so he became one of us, marvelling at the spectacle provided by the stars on show.

Richardson's delivery of the week's news is iconic. The setting, the food, the way he held up *La Gazzetta dello Sport.* It was a cool nonchalance that was not typical of football broadcasting. Richard Keys's technicolour dinner jackets were nowhere to be seen. He felt like a fan too. This wasn't a job. It was a 'how on earth have I got here' sort of style. Probably the way that audience members would've reacted in that position too. Whatever his thought process was, it worked.

One thing that didn't really take off was the use of Gazza as *Gazzetta* front man. At first, Gazza was the showpiece in the *Gazzetta* jigsaw, but quickly this turned into a problem. His difficulty in remembering and delivering lines, coupled with his tardiness and genuine shyness in front of the camera meant changes were needed. So, instead of fronting up the show as had been originally planned, he would rope in some unsuspecting Serie A stars to perform in various skits for it.

Gazza never quite hit the heights in Italy and Daniel Storey explained in his book *Gazza in Italy* how *Gazzetta* gave the player 'a link back to England outside of his fleeting international appearances'. In what was a challenging time for Gazza mentally and physically, the sheer joy and abandon of those television appearances is a far cry from the managed social media content of modern players. It does show how much the media surrounding a player plays such a vital role in maintaining a relevant profile.

Another player who had made the journey abroad a year earlier was David Platt. He joined big-spending Bari in 1991, but for the 1992/93 season joined Baggio at Italy's most successful club: Juventus. With an eye on keeping his profile high now he was playing in another country, Platt was involved in many *Gazzetta* programmes, from cooking a meal in his kitchen while talking about Juventus's fortunes to dressing up as the Terminator.

The visibility of Serie A was picked up by the football weeklies like *Shoot* and *Match* who capitalised on the interest and started to run features to get viewers up to speed on players, managers and teams. Platt made sure he was involved in this too, giving *Shoot* a club-by-club guide to Serie A. He even predicted that his own side would finish top of the pile. This was a time when football magazines offered a cursory glance around the globe. Access to a league like Serie A sowed the seeds for the access we have now to a truly global sport.

Football Italia affected a generation of football fans. A generation that has seen football grow exponentially to a game unrecognisable from the one in 1992. What could have become cult weekend viewing, flourished in the mainstream. The joys of football were embedded in the fabric of the game and the television experience. Colours and sounds burst out of the television and made the spectacle breathe. The fact that the experienced voices of Brackley and Wolstenholme commentated on these games just feels so British. James Richardson's delivery only added to that feeling.

The *Football Italia* years brought the best players in the world into British fans' living rooms. Coupled with the creation and expansion of the Champions League, there was more football on the end of a remote control than ever before. It also served to push English football in the direction of a game that would embrace players from all over the world.

Just as the Premier League was a catalyst for increased media coverage of football in England, the introduction of Italian football to terrestrial television viewers was momentous. Having access to football without a subscription or Sky dish at the time was appealing to viewers. Pay-per-view style television was still in its infancy, and loss-making, so a lot of viewers used to their four channels were understandably sceptical. *Football Italia* certainly proved that there was an appetite for more football in the home and played a huge part in the football boom of the 1990s.

9

Battle of the Roses: Leeds win the battle, United win the war

FOOTBALL RIVALRY is one of the pillars that the game is built on. Local rivalries, league rivalries, historic rivalries because of player signings and even rivalries with teams from abroad are the lifeblood of the game.

Some rivalries are flimsy. Others are circumstantial. The best are built on a legacy of intense competition.

What makes rivalries so special are those memorable moments in crucial games, when players put themselves in the spotlight and become a hero. Footballers can thrive in these games too. Putting a mark on a game against fierce rivals can etch your name into the memories of fans forever.

Two cities linked by the vivid history of their counties, Yorkshire and Lancashire, have been rivals since the Wars of the Roses during the 15th century. Obviously, organised league football was a pipe dream at that point, but you get the idea. Two regions in competition with one another to take the throne. Rivalry doesn't get bigger than this – a tagline which I'm sure has been used on a television station to describe these teams. Even the boom of the Industrial Revolution caused conflict as Leeds and Manchester tried to outdo each other. Whether it was the output of their mills or their approach to architecture, they were intertwined.

Skip forward to the 1950s and Manchester United had become one of the most successful clubs in England with a string of league titles. They were becoming a force in Europe until the Munich air disaster robbed them of the 'Busby Babes'. Leeds were a Second Division side that made it into the top flight halfway through the decade. There, they were not as competitive as they had hoped, resulting in relegation by 1960.

In the early 60s, United were in their own period of rebuilding as Busby tried to create a second generation of 'Babes'. Over the Pennines, Don Revie found himself in the hot seat at Elland Road with the task of bringing Leeds back into the First Division and making them a force. Both managers had their work cut out but believed that good coaching and developing your own players was the way to win.

During this period the clubs were intrinsically linked; Bobby Charlton's brother Jack was the rock at the heart of the Leeds defence and Johnny Giles, who would become a Leeds legend, signed from Manchester United in 1963. Giles played alongside Billy Bremner and they created one of the most fearsome midfield duos in England. The years which followed were about to provide some classic encounters and title races that would only further the rivalry.

Over the decade, both clubs competed for honours at the top of the table. The 1960s ended up belonging to Manchester United as they lifted two First Division titles to one for Revie's men. To better that even further, Busby's team finally won the European Cup in 1968 with a triumphant performance against Benfica. It would be in the 1970s that the two clubs' paths would diverge. Revie made Leeds into one of the most feared teams in Europe. The aggressive, uncompromising style upset a lot of commentators, including future Leeds manager Brian Clough, but Revie was unrepentant. The manager had fashioned a team that obsessed over the opposition. He created dossiers examining the strengths and weaknesses of every team, which meant his players knew how to tackle anyone.

Manchester United were in decline, watching on as Leeds spent a decade in the top four. For them, a perfect storm of Busby's move to the directors' box, Bobby Charlton's retirement, the inexplicable sale of Denis Law to rivals Manchester City and George Best's descent into alcoholism meant they ended up in the Second Division by 1974. All thanks to a Denis Law goal. The football gods are real, don't let anyone tell you differently.

Once Revie was replaced by Brian Clough, the glory days were over for Leeds. Manchester United ended up back in the top flight after one season and quickly got to work getting back up to the top of the table, but their path was blocked by a dominant Liverpool side and upstarts like Clough's Nottingham Forest.

By the early 80s, Manchester United had become a side that excelled in cup formats but could never sustain a successful title-winning campaign. On the other side of the rivalry, Leeds were mired in the Second Division, and ended up spending almost a decade out of the top flight. It would take the appointment of two very determined managers to get both clubs back where they belonged.

Alex Ferguson arrived in Manchester in November 1986 with a big reputation in Scotland and the trophies to prove it. He was strict and expected the players to be fit, work hard, and give everything to the cause. Something that he did not necessarily feel was present when he arrived.

Two years later, Howard Wilkinson took over Leeds from the legendary Billy Bremner. Having overachieved with an unfashionable Sheffield Wednesday side, Wilkinson dropped down to the Second Division to have a go at making Leeds great again. Like Ferguson, the new Leeds boss was a forthright figure in the dugout. His nickname: Sergeant Wilko.

By the end of the 80s, Ferguson had not yet been able to replicate the success he had achieved at Aberdeen. A second-place finish in 1987/88 was followed by mid-table finishes in the following two seasons. Even after £7m was spent to strengthen the squad, Ferguson's side could only muster a 13th-place finish in 1989/90. Winning the FA Cup saved his job, which he even admitted himself. In the same season, Leeds emerged victorious in the Second Division, finishing top on goal difference. They didn't care, they were back where they felt they belonged.

Both teams finished in the top six in the penultimate season of the First Division with Leeds finishing the higher of the two rivals. Manchester United, returning to Europe thanks to their FA Cup win, went all the way to the Cup Winners' Cup Final and defeated Johan Cruyff's Barcelona to secure Ferguson's second trophy in as many seasons. Coupled with the team's sixth-place finish, it was clear that they were going to be a force.

During this period, Ferguson had been slowly rebuilding the spine of the side that he had taken over from Ron Atkinson. Out went Paul McGrath, Norman Whiteside and Gordon Strachan and in came Gary Pallister, Paul Ince and Steve Bruce. These three players would form the backbone of the team that would go on to dominate the Premier League in its infancy.

Leeds were the beneficiary of Strachan being cast aside by Ferguson. He proved to be an inspiration at Elland Road and continued to perform at a high level in the First Division. Wilkinson surrounded him with young midfielders Gary Speed and David Batty, while Gary McAllister provided the class that knitted the four players together. Lee Chapman was the other star player in the side. He had served under Sergeant Wilko at Sheffield Wednesday and after a few years away, joined his old boss in the Second Division. Now a First Division striker, he backed up his performances with a bucketload of goals, scoring 31 in all competitions in the 1990/91 season that saw Leeds finish fourth.

So, to the 1991/92 season and a series of events that set in motion the creation of a dynasty that would dominate the Premier League era. No other club has had the domestic success that Manchester United have enjoyed since 1992, but the building blocks had been put in place by Ferguson from the moment he joined the club, removing the all-encompassing drinking culture, bringing in younger, hungrier players, transforming the mentality around the club and investing in the spine of his team.

Around the league, the once-dominant Liverpool had embarked on an extended period of rebuilding, whether they knew it or not. Arsenal were the best team in the league, having won the title on the back of just one defeat all season. George Graham signed Ian Wright for £2.5m, which meant they had one of the best strike forces in the league. Promoted Sheffield Wednesday under Trevor Francis were hoping to follow Leeds' example by competing at the top end of the table.

Throughout his tenure as United manager, Ferguson was not afraid to spend. In his book *Alex Ferguson: 6 Years at United*, he complained that the media saw him as a big-spending manager, but after spending £12m and not delivering a title, maybe they were right. Alternatively, Ferguson was trying to find the right balance in his squad to ensure they could compete in the long term.

The summer of 1991 brought the arrival of two more players who would become first-team regulars and vital cogs in what was becoming a well-oiled machine.

Peter Schmeichel solved the troublesome goalkeeper position for United immediately. He could have had a whole chapter dedicated to how he changed modern football with his innovative and much-copied brand of goalkeeping. Initially, Ferguson had sent his goalkeeping coach Alan Hodgkinson to watch Schmeichel in a range of international and club games. The verdict was to the point: the Dane was the best goalkeeper in Europe. A deal was quickly agreed and United had their new man for £550,000.

The next signing that summer was linked to the new UEFA rule of only allowing four foreign players in the squad for European games. United had Irishmen, Welshmen and Scots throughout the starting line-up so the need for English players was paramount. One player that piqued Ferguson's interest was Paul Parker. He was English and an excellent defender. After beating off other clubs' interest, Ferguson signed him for £1.7m. It was the final piece in the jigsaw that would create the legendary back five: Schmeichel, Parker, Irwin, Bruce and Pallister.

The team was set for a title onslaught. In attack, Mark Hughes and Brian McClair provided the firepower while new sensation Ryan Giggs provided the width alongside recent signing Andrei Kanchelskis and United's other wonderkid, Lee Sharpe. Ince, Webb and Robson would provide the steel and creativity in a competitive midfield. Ferguson was confident that after success in Europe his team would be able to pass the ultimate test and win the league.

Leeds were buoyed by their fourth-place finish on their return to the First Division. Not content with just maintaining their position, they spend over £4m adding to the squad. The nucleus of Wilkinson's side was bolstered by the arrivals of Rod and Ray Wallace from Southampton (the third brother, Danny, was still at Manchester United), defenders Jon Newsome, David Weatherall and Tony Dorigo with Steve Hodge adding experience and depth to Leeds' already strong midfield. Hodge and Rod Wallace proved to be excellent signings and their goals took the burden off Chapman, who was the talisman of the side. Wilkinson was confident that his team had a chance of doing well that season.

Fergie's side made a brilliant start to the campaign. Unbeaten until October, their early form included a five-game winning streak that showed off the quality of the squad, especially defensively. New additions

Schmeichel and Parker formed part of a unit that kept eight clean sheets until that first defeat, which came against Wilkinson's former club Sheffield Wednesday.

Leeds' first defeat also came in October, but a couple of weeks earlier. The two teams matched each other stride for stride in those first three months of the season, with both recording eight wins. Having played an extra game, Leeds accumulated one more point to sit top of the table. Both teams were superb in the league leading up to Christmas. This title race was, on the face of it, going right down to the wire. There were other teams involved in it too, but none could match Manchester United and Leeds for strength in depth.

Behind the scenes, while the title race was in full flow, plans were being made for the new Premier League, but that was irrelevant when these teams were competing. Interestingly, Alex Ferguson was quite an outspoken advocate of the status quo at the time. Considering the dominance that was on the horizon for his team, Ferguson did not want to change the structure of the leagues and was particularly disappointed by the move to show games on a Monday night.

This Manchester United team was experiencing fixture congestion at first hand during the season as they progressed in cup competitions. In fact, they had played nine cup games by the end of 1991 compared to five for Leeds. Fixture congestion is something that would plague Manchester United at the end of the season and ultimately go towards their failure to lift the league title.

One of those additional games was against Red Star Belgrade in the European Super Cup. Emerging triumphant against a very talented side, it was another trophy in the cabinet for Ferguson who, despite a lot of criticism for not delivering a league title, was establishing United on the European stage again.

As football developed over this period, the fixture calendar changed dramatically. Specific breaks were given for international football, avoiding arguments with managers about releasing players; the European competitions were given specific nights and league fixtures were rearranged to accommodate this. These are practices that still exist today and despite managers' constant discussion of playing too many games, or games in quick succession, spare a thought for the teams of the early 90s.

With 1992 on the horizon, United and Leeds faced off in the league. They were also drawn against each other in both domestic cup competitions; the FA Cup and the Rumbelows League Cup. Three fixtures at Elland Road ended up with a draw in the league and Manchester United victorious in the two cup games. In contrast to the games in the previous season, there was little to no trouble on and off the pitch. Ferguson believed that his opposite number had helped to establish Leeds once again as a big club and gave him credit for their improved play and behaviour.

Both teams continued to motor through their league campaigns with barely a defeat in sight. Consistency was key and in the early part of 1992 the teams lost one game each – in January for Manchester United and February for Leeds. As the season moved on, both sides' form dipped slightly, and they traded places at the top of the table.

The transfer window as we know it today, and its non-stop coverage on TV, is a modern invention. Fans love to see who their clubs are trying to sign as it increases their excitement and hope that their team are just about to turn the corner and see the bright lights of success waiting for them. There had always been a transfer window in England, but the difference was it lasted all season, only closing on 31 March. Deadline-day signings were still made, but not really with the same fanfare as they are today. Clubs would often sign players during the season but, unlike today, they would not remodel a whole team. Instead, the final piece of the jigsaw could be added or even a replacement brought in to cover an unexpected injury. Most teams were happy to do their business in the summer and see the season out. Compare that with today when there have been instances of clubs spending huge amounts of money mid-season.

Leeds dipped into the transfer market to bolster their charge for the title on 4 February 1992. The player was Eric Cantona. An era-defining moment, but not for the team that bought him.

Cantona was a controversial figure before he even arrived in the First Division. For Leeds, his contribution was vital, even if he was restricted to six starts. Most of his appearances came from the bench where he had the chance to change the game. Cantona did just that, scoring important goals and creating chances for others, especially Chapman. His impact was immediate and vital. Manchester United, on the other hand, did not address their failings in attack. Consistently linked with a move for Southampton striker Alan Shearer, nothing materialised and they went with what they had.

United entered the final stretch of the season in front. They had already secured victory in the League Cup against Nottingham Forest and hoped to take that form into the remaining league games. Leeds had lost 4-0 to Manchester City so needed to quickly regroup. The final five games defined the season. For Manchester United, these games were condensed into 14 days whereas Leeds' games were played out over 21 days. It was an extraordinary end to the season, thanks to Manchester United's extended runs in the cups.

Incredibly, considering how consistent they had been all season, Ferguson's side lost three games in a row to Forest, West Ham and Liverpool. It ended their chance of winning the title as Leeds triumphed in games against Coventry City and Sheffield United in the same period. Howard Wilkinson had led the team to the Second Division title just two years earlier and now had secured the last ever First Division crown.

The memory of that Leeds team is of determination, organisation and an incredible team ethic. McAllister, Speed, Strachan and Batty all made names for themselves as one of the best midfield units in the league. But throughout the team players had career-best seasons and consistency that took them over the finish line. The added flair of Cantona towards the end of the campaign merely galvanised an already great team.

Leaving a legacy is a different story. Wilkinson's men could not build on their title-winning season, instead finishing 17th in the inaugural Premier League. There was a real chance of relegation that season, but luckily, they saw off the danger and managed to stay up. They bounced back with two fifth-place finishes in 1993/94 and 1994/95 but returned to mid table soon after.

Wilkinson left to be replaced with George Graham, who followed the same mid-table/top five path of his predecessor. The football at times was dour. The signing of Jimmy Floyd Hasselbaink solved their goalscoring problems and he would excel over his two seasons at the club. Incredibly, Graham decided to leave Leeds for Spurs after the sacking of Christian Gross. David O'Leary took over and the dream began again for Leeds.

Huge investment was pumped into the club to buy new players and compete at the top of what was becoming one of the richest leagues in the world. Champions League adventures featuring players brought through from the youth team conjured up ideas of competing for the title once again. Harry Kewell, Mark Viduka, Michael Bridges, Rio Ferdinand, Alan Smith and the like developed a strong bond with the fans and neutrals alike. The period brought Leeds back to relevance on the European stage as had been the case under Revie. The problem was, along the M62 things had gone a bit differently for Manchester United.

Ultimately, they had struggled for goals towards the end of the campaign. They had scored 42 goals up to the turn of the year, but only managed 21 in the second half. Ferguson knew that he needed to bring in a striker so he set about trying to sign the best one he could. The search led him, and many other clubs, to Alan Shearer. The young striker had a growing reputation and had come off his best scoring season for Southampton. Added to that, he had been integrated into the England setup by Graham Taylor and been selected for the 1992 European Championships. At 21 he was the youngest player in the squad and by some seen as the long-term replacement for Gary Lineker.

Blackburn Rovers, a team with the money to challenge at the top of the Premier League, and Manchester United were in a two-horse race to sign Shearer. Southampton knew that they held all the cards and would demand a British record transfer fee for him. Both teams were desperate to sign the striker and Ferguson usually got his man.

However, not confident about the large sum being asked for the player, United backed down and Blackburn were able to secure the signing for anywhere between £3.3m and £3.6m, depending on which reports you read. Blackburn owner Jack Walker stated that he wanted to make United 'look cheap' and as the Premier League season started, he had certainly done that. Blackburn had spent millions in the summer to ensure they were not just competing to keep their place in the league.

The transfer business at Old Trafford in the summer of 1992 featured the signing of one player: Dion Dublin. Part of a Cambridge United side under John Beck that roared up the league in a similar way to Watford and Wimbledon in the 80s, Dublin was a lean, tall striker and certainly not a similar style to Shearer. He rejected the advances of Chelsea to sign for United in the hope of a run at the Premier League title.

The signing was a surprise, but for £1m Ferguson hoped that he had the right player to prevent his team misfiring in front of goal. Events of the first few weeks of the new season would be defining in the history of Manchester United and change everything for them and their place in English football.

On 2 September 1992, Dublin broke his leg against Crystal Palace, a week after scoring the winner in United's first victory of the season. He would be out for six months. United's hope for the 1992/93 season was hanging by a thread and so Ferguson would again have to dip into the transfer market to fill the hole up front. By the time Dublin broke his leg, Shearer had scored four goals in his first five games for Blackburn.

Another striker that had been on Ferguson's wish list before Dublin was Sheffield Wednesday's David Hirst. He had monitored him during the back end of the 1991/92 season and made a move for him in the summer before having his bid rejected by Trevor

Francis. With Dublin's injury, Ferguson made his move again.

At the time, Hirst was a highly rated striker scoring plenty of goals for Sheffield Wednesday, so he had pedigree in the First Division. By this point in his career he had scored more goals than Shearer. The striker had also been capped by his country. One thing stood in Hirst's way: Trevor Francis. Multiple offers were made by United but Francis stood firm. United's offer was well over £3m and some reports suggested it would have broken the record set by Shearer. According to the Wednesday manager, Ferguson even gave Francis his famed hairdryer treatment down the phone. It didn't make any difference and so Ferguson was back to square one.

By late October, United's league form was proving to be a problem. After a five-game winning streak, they had now drawn five in a row. Clearly, they were not over the problems of the previous season and things didn't look like they were changing anytime soon. The powers that be knew that they needed to do something, so they drew up a list of targets.

While in a meeting about who they could sign, Martin Edwards's phone rang. Bill Fotherby was

Leeds' managing director and he wanted to know if there was a possibility that Leeds could re-sign Denis Irwin. The Irishman was a solid performer for United in a strong back line. He was integral to what Ferguson was building and so Edwards gave the suggestion short shrift.

On the list of striking targets was Chapman, so Edwards asked Fotherby if the Englishman was available, ignoring the fact he was Leeds' main goalscorer. At the same time, Ferguson was scribbling the name of Cantona on a piece of paper. Edwards duly asked the questions and Fotherby promised a reply within the day.

They didn't wait that long and within an hour the deal was underway.

Incredibly, all parties agreed terms and the transfer fee very quickly. Manchester United's total outlay for Cantona was £1.2m. Considering the Frenchman was signed from their main rival for the title the previous season, the fee seems ludicrous. They had money to spend after the failed pursuit of Shearer and Hirst, so why Leeds did not hold out for a higher fee is anyone's guess. Ferguson didn't care as he knew Cantona could be the catalyst for his team.

Ferguson was delighted with the signing and knew that Cantona could tip the title chase in United's favour as he had done for Leeds the season before. All the incidents that had plagued him in France (including insulting his national coach, fighting with team-mates and calling members of a disciplinary committee 'idiots') had given him a poor reputation as a player, but one thing Cantona did have was a will to win. That was what he cared about. He wanted the opportunity to play and show the United fans what he was all about.

The figure of Sir Matt Busby loomed large at Old Trafford in 1992 and Ferguson understood that emulating his legacy was vital. While Ferguson was spending money on players in his first six years in charge at United, he was also building on and improving the infrastructure of the club. A key part of United's DNA was youth. He wrote in his book *Alex Ferguson: 6 Years at United* that he felt immense pride and inspiration to 'achieve the vision Sir Matt Busby always had for Manchester United'.

At that point, United only had 14 players over the age of 25 on their books: youth was the priority. He knew the importance of giving an opportunity to younger players and had already done so with Lee Sharpe, his son Darren and a wonderkid from Wales in the form of Ryan Giggs. Sharpe had played his way into the team superbly after his arrival from Torquay United. In a similar position on the pitch, Giggs just arrived, almost fully formed as one of the most exciting players in football. Both offered a glimpse of what Ferguson thought United could be.

After losing the league title in 1992, there was one title that United won that year that really did change football. With a sharp focus on youth, United had developed a group of players that blossomed in the early 1990s, culminating in a squad full of players with the potential for long professional careers. The youth team setup was managed by Eric Harrison, who had some frank discussions with Ferguson at the start of his reign about the number of players coming through the youth ranks. The manager was not content with one or two a season – he wanted more.

So, Ferguson expanded the scouting network at the club to ensure that United could attract and sign the best youth players from around the country. He knew this would strengthen the whole club and provide him with players well versed in the United system. This vision and blueprint paid off with the group of players that emerged under Harrison.

Gary Neville, Nicky Butt, David Beckham and Ryan Giggs: four Manchester United legends in the same squad. Keith Gillespie and Robbie Savage, two Premier League stalwarts. Ben Thornley, Kevin Pilkington, Chris Casper, John O'Kane, Simon Davies and Colin McKee all made it as professional footballers. It was an incredible achievement to produce so many players from one club. The following season, Phil Neville and Paul Scholes were added to the group. Fergie had his fledglings, ready to emulate Busby.

That group of players came together to win the Youth Cup in 1992, defeating Crystal Palace 6-3 on aggregate. Two excellent performances from Harrison's team got the group into the national newspapers. Everyone tipped the squad for stardom with so many 'can't miss' prospects. Ferguson even said himself that if these players did not make it then everyone might as well go home.

Ironically, the following season the same group of players, with the younger Neville and Scholes now full members of the squad, lost to Leeds United in the Youth Cup Final. Jamie Forrester, Noel Whelan and Mark Tinkler were the stars for Paul Hart's team, but those three young men did not have the same impact as United's group. It will be hard for any team to match such an incredible group of youth players coming together like that at one club.

There was, of course, luck involved with producing so many professionals in one group, but that does not mean it was not undertaken by design. Ferguson knew that all strong clubs produce their own. Other clubs made shrewd signings and built squads through the transfer market, but he wanted the United blueprint to be as it was in the 50s and 60s. Next in the plan would be finding a way to integrate them within the first team.

Over the rest of the 1990s, Ferguson found space for those youth team players. Neville became a fixture in defence, Giggs, Scholes, Butt and Beckham would've been a title-winning midfield alone, but the fact that Roy Keane signed in 1993 strengthened the side even further. Losing Bryan Robson to Middlesbrough in 1994 and Paul Ince to Inter Milan in 1995 didn't stop the United train motoring.

Ferguson knew all about his young players. He knew their families, their habits, and their best and worst qualities. Neville wrote in his autobiography *Red* that Ferguson 'knew our games and our characters inside out'. Risking huge financial outlay on a player that might not adapt to their new surroundings was not what Ferguson wanted to do. He needed players with the attitude required to take United on and win. And win they did.

When Cantona signed for United in November 1992, they sat sixth in the table, nine points off leaders Norwich. They had already lost four games, only two less than the previous season. After his debut as a substitute in a 2-1 win against Manchester City, United would only lose two more games. They were crowned champions after Aston Villa's 1-0 defeat at home at the hands of struggling Oldham Athletic. The 26-year wait for a league title had ended and United were about to embark on a trophy-laden decade that changed the club's standing in English football.

Cantona galvanised United and provided the spark they needed to build up a run of good form that would ultimately take them to the title. He finished the league season with 15 goals for Leeds and Manchester United combined. Nine of his goals came for the latter, but it was his link-up play and skill that added an extra dimension to the team. On his arrival, Brian McClair moved back into midfield so Cantona could play up front. After Keane signed to partner Ince in midfield, McClair dropped to the bench so Cantona and Hughes became the full-time partnership in attack.

The next four seasons would produce three more league titles. Shearer's Blackburn won a single title in 1994/95 to stop total domination. United were the leading club in England and were focused on removing Liverpool from their perch as the most successful club domestically.

Surely one of the best signings ever made in the Premier League, Cantona's influence on the fabric of the club was huge. Not just on the pitch, but his influence on the younger players to put in the hard yards in training in order to improve, set those players, and the club, on a path of unmatched success.

Of course, there were some significant issues with Cantona that had been well publicised before he arrived in England. Leeds fans were not exposed to this as the Manchester United fans were in his performances against Galatasaray and a baying mob of police and opposition fans. The infamous kung-fu kick at Crystal Palace in January 1995 certainly did not enhance his reputation outside of Manchester, but at Old Trafford they knew how much they would miss their talisman, who was banned for nine months by the FA. It is no coincidence that the only time United didn't win a title in the Cantona era was that 1994/95 season. Ferguson stood by his player and knew that he would be key to their future.

During this time, it was Ferguson's single-minded desire to win that powered the team on. He was a great man-manager, especially of experienced players. Added to his careful management of the youth team players, it was a potent mix. His squad were trained, conditioned almost, to play a certain way for United and nothing would get in their way. Later, United players would reveal how this had a detrimental impact on the England team of that era. Successful players just found it difficult to win alongside their bitter rivals.

As well as carefully embedding youth team players into the senior side for the first time, United bought players that fitted their system, often weakening their rivals in the process. They broke the domestic transfer record to sign Roy Keane in 1993, and then spent

£6m on Andy Cole from Newcastle in January 1995, sending the £1m-rated Keith Gillespie north as part of the deal. Keegan's side were playing in the upper reaches of the Premier League but could not turn down an offer of that magnitude.

By this time, money was flowing into the game and United were one of the biggest beneficiaries. Merchandising, television rights and sponsorships grew exponentially for the club, resulting in huge revenue. The development of Old Trafford meant that more spectators could fit into the stadium and the increased footfall meant more visitors to the club shop. Matchdays were slowly starting to become an experience, rather than a chance to watch a match.

Success on the pitch also helped develop United as a global brand. Winning four of the first five Premier League titles gave them instant recognition around the world as the best team in England. Although they were not instantly successful in the Champions League, the new group format meant guaranteed income from television rights and more exposure in a wide range of nations.

The key players during this period were Cantona, Keane and Fergie's Fledglings. Like a changing of the guard, the young players took up the mantle of first-teamers from 1995 and despite ridicule from the press, became a title-winning squad. Schmeichel and Irwin had been part of the side that was so close to claiming the league title in 1991/92, but now they were the elder statesmen of the team.

Ferguson, front and centre through it all, had become the best manager in the country and one of the most highly rated in Europe. He had built the club back up to a position of total domestic dominance. United played exciting, attacking football, in keeping with what Ferguson saw as the United way. A relentless drive and quest for success meant that players gave everything for the team and wanted to win at all costs. The players reflected the qualities of their manager.

Europe was an area that Ferguson and United struggled to conquer. The finances and resources available to teams on the continent still far outweighed those in the Premier League. He also had to deal with the retirement of Eric Cantona after lifting another title in 1997. The departure left a hole in the side to be filled by Teddy Sheringham from Spurs. It would be Spurs' rivals Arsenal that took the league title in 1998, working away at United to bring down the reigning champions' lead. Ferguson would finish the season empty handed. The following year would make up for it.

By the time the 1998/99 season came around, Ferguson was ready to spend to strengthen. Jaap Stam signed for a then club record £10m, which was soon broken with the arrival of Dwight Yorke from Aston Villa for £12.6m. These fees were less than those spent in 1992 on Vialli, in Stam's case, and Lentini, in Yorke's. English teams were starting to reap the rewards of the Premier League money tree, but still had quite a way to go to compete with the billionaires of Europe.

It was to be the peak of Ferguson's time at United. After all the team-building in the late 80s, and the blooding of youngsters in the 90s, finally the ultimate European trophy was secured. A last-ditch victory in the Champions League Final against Bayern Munich on a memorable night in the Nou Camp, crowned the end of the 90s as the decade that belonged to United. Like Liverpool from the mid-70s to late 80s, United had totally dominated domestically. The Premier League was their trophy. Everyone wanted a piece of them, much to the constant annoyance of

Ferguson, who bemoaned teams having their best game against United.

All this dominance came from some key decisions made by Ferguson during his early years at the club. Investing in that scouting network to find the best youth team players across the country, changing the social culture of the dressing room and ultimately buying Eric Cantona. These events came together perfectly in 1992. Although they weren't league champions in that calendar year, the Youth Cup triumph and signing of Cantona set United up for dominance that stretched past Cantona's retirement in 1997, the Champions League triumph in 1999 and well into the 2010s as Ferguson's tenure at United came to an end.

On and off the pitch, United became the richest and most successful club in the world by the end of the 1990s. They had utilised a youth setup as a conveyor belt for the first team that clubs like Barcelona would emulate with their La Masia academy to bring their own level of success. Commercial prosperity was achieved through huge merchandising and sponsorship deals while providing a quality product on the pitch. Clubs like Real Madrid attempted to increase their commercial prospects with the Galacticos transfer policy and in Italy, Lazio bought up every European star they could get their hands on.

But, in 1992, after finishing second best to Howard Wilkinson's Leeds, Manchester United emerged as a forward-thinking club in the early years of the modern game.

10

Legacy: Where are we now?

A YEAR is a long time, but the events of 1992 left an
indelible mark on football. The actions and changes
in that year shaped the game fans watch today. From
involving goalkeepers in attacking play, competing
against the best teams in Europe in the Champions
League and the vast sums of money spent on transfers,
all of this can be traced back to 92. Modern football
in its current form was born here.

Detractors will say that football before 1992
should not be ignored. That is true. Players and
teams from generations earlier should be lauded for
their incredible achievements and innovations. There
is a wealth of football history that is untapped for
a modern audience. Although the past should be
revered, a clear line in the sand was drawn during

this period. Changes happened quickly and at times no one stopped to think. Measuring modern achievements from 1992 onwards does, most of the time, make sense. There are so many factors involved that make the game different.

Altering the back-pass rule was a huge shift in the way football would be played. Comparing the pre- and post-1992 eras is difficult when you consider the choice that players had to pass back to the goalkeeper. This was not some minor alteration to the offside rule. It marked a shift in what outfield players were able to do. Before the rule change, managers used the tactic as part of their match planning. A way to run down the clock at the end of the game. Bringing a rule like this into force was probably the best invention in the modern game. More so than the influx of money, better coaches or fitter, more athletic players. This rule change was like the changes made to the hand-checking rule in basketball. Fundamentally the sport is different.

Off the pitch, ownership in football changed hugely with the introduction of the Premier League and the Champions League. Both competitions sought to line the pockets of clubs with television revenue that would see money pour in. Now, a select group of clubs were able to hoover up talent at a phenomenal rate, especially as the rules around EU players changed.

With huge sums of money involved in football, the type of owner changed. Bernard Tapie and Silvio Berlusconi had been seen as outliers, men who wanted a club as a hobby or plaything, whereas most of the others were company men, content to keep their clubs afloat and turning over enough revenue to develop a playing squad that competed. As times changed, so did the men in the boardroom. The vision of these men was to squash their domestic leagues into submission and manipulate European competition to further serve their (financial) domination.

Using the explosion of interest in football after Italia 90, television companies and their owners seized on the new shiny football product and spread it around the world. This was where the money would be made. They were right. Much of the income of the world's wealthiest clubs came through worldwide revenue, driven by television deals.

In England, the negotiation of the television deal was a cornerstone on which the new Premier League was built. The idea of bringing down the number of competitive games for English clubs, to help the national team improve and maintain its place amongst the elite after Italia 90, quickly disappeared when money became involved. A super league was indeed created with the revenues to match.

The legacy of the rush for television cash has meant wall-to-wall coverage of football in the modern era. Sky Sports has dedicated channels to football and the Premier League and Sky Sports News relentlessly plays clips from games, speculates about transfers, and uses ex-players as pundits to shed light on the day's issues. Of course, these things are not new, and have always formed part of the game, but now they drive the issues rather than report or reflect on them.

In truth, the modern game would not be what it is without the explosion of finance brought into the game in the 90s. The Premier League was a significant catalyst for this change, but similar financial boosts were appearing in various locations across the continent. More teams spent large sums to be involved in games with growing audiences. After all, the public only wants to see the best players.

Now, the Champions League has become a homogenised set of matches that may feature the best players but at times feature no real jeopardy. Instead, this must be created by the television channels through promotional material and storylines built around a game. The language used is burned into the football lexicon. Phrases like 'Super Sunday' or 'The Big Six' are synonymous with football in England, to a point where you almost don't need to question what they mean.

The shift meant wealth coming into clubs like Chelsea, via Roman Abramovich, Manchester City with Sheik Mansour and now Newcastle United and the Saudi Arabian PIF. Clubs that were on the outside when the Premier League was formed, are now very much on the inside thanks to their huge wealth.

Players have been significant beneficiaries of these changes too. The exposure given by constantly televised games has allowed them to become celebrities outside of the football world. Footballers had always been famous, but more in their local high street or, if they were lucky, in adverts and television appearances.

David Beckham paved the way by marrying a Spice Girl and setting up brand deals with elite names. He was not just content with stardom on the pitch, his brand was well and truly alive off it. More players followed suit with lucrative brand deals that dwarfed the finances available before 1992. The days of players owning newsagents and post offices are long gone. Now, they have management companies sourcing lucrative entertainment or business ventures throughout their career, which prepares them for life after football.

For some, the riches are so great that they will never work again. Of course, the top players from the past were rewarded handsomely relative to the average earner. Footballers are no longer earning three or four times more than a member of the public, but exponentially more. Players are almost their own financial ecosystem, even supporting other members of the family with their wealth. It is not uncommon to see players investing in properties and businesses for their closest associates.

The man that made sure BSkyB won the Premier League television deal, Alan Sugar, was right when he warned that all this TV money would end up in the players' and not owners' hands. Players have all the power from their ironclad contracts that offer huge remuneration and bonuses on top. Some are starting to have a voice with ownership groups too, which can only spell disaster.

Those players that moved in 1992 for vast sums of money had varied fortunes on the pitch and in the intervening years. The three players who commanded record transfer fees – Jean-PierrePapin, Gianluca Vialli and Guanluisi Lentini – certainly didn't become legends of the world game. Vialli had the biggest impact on Juventus, winning a league title and a Champions League, but it's probably his time later at Chelsea as a player and then manager that made more of a mark. The number of foreign players increased rapidly in the Premier League, but particularly at Chelsea, with Vialli and his predecessor Ruud Gullit at the forefront. Once Vialli became player/manager he even fielded a line-up that did not feature any UK-based players, a change which was not foreseen in 1992.

Vialli and his move to Chelsea typified the changing landscape in England thanks to the Premier League. No longer seen as an unattractive proposition by players from the continent thanks to the style of football, international players flooded the newly minted league. When Vialli arrived at Stamford Bridge in 1996, clubs' spending was rising dramatically. In that same summer, Fabrizio Ravanelli signed for Middlesbrough for £7m and became the highest-paid player in the league on a rumoured £42,000 a week. Soon after Euro 96, Alan Shearer was considered one of the best strikers in the world and the £15m fee paid by Newcastle dwarfed the Ravanelli deal. Four years earlier Shearer had become the British record transfer for Blackburn. Kenny Dalglish had used Jack Walker's wallet to buy Shearer for £3.3m and now his value had gone up over 400 per cent. The mid-90s really were the days when football became removed from the way it was a decade earlier.

Spending on players was the way that clubs got fans into the stadiums. It also meant that people would want to watch them on television around the world. Some clubs invested shrewdly while others chased the dream, got burned and soon found their way down the divisions.

The spending obviously continued as the television deals increased to the point where 25 years after Alan Shearer's record-breaking deal, Neymar was transferred from Barcelona to Paris Saint-Germain for £200m. An eye-watering sum of money that will possibly never be topped. They said the same about the grotesque sums of money being spent in Italy in the summer of 92, so maybe some things will never change.

There have been too many huge transfers to mention over the last 30-plus years, but one thing that has not changed is the financial dominance of the biggest teams in the world. The rich have certainly got richer, in society and in football, and anyone who tries to threaten that dominance must be quashed.

As mentioned, clubs like Manchester City, Newcastle United and PSG have enjoyed huge cash injections from nation states. They have too much power to be challenged, but when other clubs have tried to spend to make it into the big time they have ultimately failed. Good management still outweighs the amount you have to spend, but the money certainly helps.

One switch that did come about was the dominance of the Premier League in all financial aspects of the game, from commercial revenue to transfers. Clubs in the Premier League dominate thanks to enormous worldwide television revenue. Now, the overseas part of the television rights deals exceeds that of the domestic rights. It is incredible to think that the Premier League was created to reduce the number of games played by exhausted footballers.

Eleven of the top 20 richest clubs in the world (as of 2021) were from the Premier League. This number has steadily increased each season as the television deal now eclipses what any other league receives. Huge growth in broadcast rights has come from the expansion into Asia and people's desire to watch every Premier League game.

Transfer spending has followed a similar path. In the 1990s, Serie A was the destination for players and coaches. The enormous transfer spending and high wages meant the best players in the world wanted to play in Italy. Most summers would be spent watching Italian clubs parading a whole team's worth of signings while in England, we marvelled at the top clubs who added three or four players (with one marquee signing) each summer.

That changed when Abramovich blew other teams out of the water with a spend of £121.5m in one summer. It was only the third time a club had ever spent over £100m and it was the first time it had happened in England. They were also the biggest spenders for a second season in a row, battling it out with Real Madrid and Florentino Perez's Galacticos vanity project to see who could spend the most.

Manchester City were the upstarts trying to break into the elite in the late 2000s. They spent over £100m trying to usurp the dominance of Manchester United/ Arsenal/Chelsea at the top of the Premier League. Mark Hughes was the man tasked with spending the money and to be honest, at first, it didn't work. Ultimately, the club succeeded in reaching the heights of Premier League glory and Champions League knockout games through sustained spending on infrastructure. the playing squad and foreign coaches.

Money has been the driving factor of success for clubs in the last 30 years. Most of the commentators and people involved in football in 1992 could see what was happening. The clubs could see it too. The problem was they wanted to be part of it. Berlusconi's wish for a European Super League away from UEFA has in effect come true. The super clubs spend the most and channel the revenue upwards. The attitude is set to spend more than the competition. It's as simple as that.

Modern football has created a system where success is tied to the size of your wage bill. UEFA did not set out to create a virtual closed shop in European competition, but when the clubs hold most of the power there is not much they can do.

That power has filtered down to the players who are extravagantly rewarded for their immense talents with super-sized contracts. To top it off for owners, Jean-Marc Bosman won the right for all players to walk away from their contract on its completion. Fans might say that is fair for players, but owners had built a system on outspending your rivals, which has proved to be unsustainable.

Football has certainly reached another crossroads. Like 1992, things do need to change and improve. Gaps are widening between the richest clubs in Europe and the rest. To some smaller teams' credit, they are trying to be more inventive and innovative. New recruitment models that prioritise team-specific skill sets are crucial in standing out from the crowd. Too often, though, these players are then swallowed up by teams with the financial muscle to win every fight.

After the coronavirus pandemic, most smaller clubs started to act differently. They are being more diligent about who they sign, investing more time in analytics and scouting to ensure that their player is the right fit for what they want. Chopping and changing whole squads of players every three years just isn't financially viable.

Bigger clubs have reverted to type. Despite the world's finances experiencing a period of turbulence, the richest clubs continue to spend extravagant amounts of money. They are so wealthy that they can keep great swathes of players out on loan as assets that can be sold to finance the first team. These shadow squads prevent other clubs from having long-term access to players who are never going to be able to play at the same level as their team-mates.

Change may well be on the horizon. UEFA are in the process of linking clubs' spending on player transfer fees and wages so that clubs do not get into a position where they mortgage their future success for the here and now. In principle, it is a great idea, but in practice it will serve to penalise smaller clubs who have very little chance of increasing revenue due to stadium size or lack of participation in Europe. Meanwhile, it will help the clubs who have been spending more money than the GDP of a small country to live within their enormous riches. A two-tiered system will almost certainly be created within the game.

Significant structural change was proposed by Europe's biggest clubs when the idea of a Super League reared its head again in April 2021, when it was announced that 12 clubs had come together to form a breakaway competition. This was not sanctioned or authorised by UEFA. It was a separate entity, a closed shop, one that would be defeated within three days. Incredibly, the project still lingers with Real Madrid, Barcelona and Juventus still involved. The fact they have no support begs the question of how long they can possibly stay affiliated with a competition that doesn't exist.

Interestingly, Sky was one of the largest organisations to argue against the prospect of the Super League. Possibly because they were not involved in the negotiations to bring this new project to television.

Clubs may well have realised that, although their coffers are bursting with money from television revenue, maybe they need to collect their earnings directly. They can set the price, collect the cash, and spend it how they wish. Maybe that is what's on the cards over the next 30 years.

There may well be another year of significant football change like there was in 1992. But there will never be a year that transforms the fundamental aspects of the game. Rule changes, a new league structure and a change in European geography collided in one incredible 12-month period.

Love it or hate it, there is a clear divide between the football before and after that year. What can't be denied is that modern football was born in 1992.

Bibliography

Books

Connolly, K. and MacWilliam, R., *Fields of Glory, Paths of Gold: The History of European Football* (Edinburgh: Mainstream Publishing Company, 2005)

Cox, M., *The Mixer – The Story of Premier League Tactics, from Route One to False Nines* (London: Harper Collins, 2017)

Cruyff, J., *My Turn – Johan Cruyff* (London: Macmillan, 2016)

Dixon, J., *The Fix: How the First Champions League Was Won and Why We All Lost* (Sussex: Pitch Publishing, 2021)

Foot, J., *Calcio – a History of Italian Football* (London: Harper Perennial, 2006)

Ferguson, A. and Meek, D., *Alex Ferguson: 6 Years at United* (Edinburgh: Mainstream Publishing Company, 1992)

Flynn, A., and Guest, L., with Law, P., *The Secret Life of Football* (London: Queen Anne Press, 1989)

Goldblatt, D., The *Ball is Round – A Global History of Football* (London: Penguin, 2006)

Goldblatt, D., *The Game of our Lives: The Meaning and Making of English Football* (London: Penguin,, 2015)

Grade, J., *Golazzo: The Football Italia Years* (London: independently published, 2020)

Radnedge, K., *50 Years of the European Cup and Champions League* (London: Carlton Books, 2005)

Robinson, J. and Clegg, J., *The Club – How the Premier League Became the Richest, Most Disruptive Business in Sport* (London: John Murray, 2019)

Robson, B., *Robbo: My Autobiography* (London: Hodder & Stoughton Ltd, 2006)

Rollin, J., *Rothmans Football Yearbook 1991–92* (London: Queen Anne Press, 1991)

Rollin, J., *Rothmans Football Yearbook 1992-93*
(London: Headline Book Publishing, 1992)

Rollin, J., *Rothmans Football Yearbook 1993-94*
(London: Headline Book Publishing, 1993)

Sacchi, A., *The Immortals: How My Milan
Team Reinvented Football* (London:
BackPage Press, 2021)

Scragg, S., *The Undisputed Champions of Europe:
How the Gods of Football Became European
Royalty* (Sussex: Pitch Publishing, 2021)

Smyth, R., Eriksen, L. and Gibbons, M., *Danish
Dynamite – The Story of Football's Greatest Cult
Team* (London: Bloomsbury, 2014)

Storey, D., *Gazza in Italy* (London: Harper
Collins, 2018)

Wilson, J., *Inverting the Pyramid – The History of
Football Tactics* (London: Orion, 2008)

Magazines

90 Minutes

European Championship 92: The Official BBC Sports Magazine

FourFourTwo

Match

Shoot

When Saturday Comes

World Soccer

Websites

BD Futbol

England Football Online

Football Reference

FourFourTwo

National Football Museum

Planet Football

Premier League

The Athletic

The Guardian

The History Boys

The Independent

These Football Times

Transfermarkt

UEFA